THE BIN

D Malone McMillan

ISBN 978-1-7320062-5-6 (paperback)
ISBN 978-1-7320062-6-3 (epub ebook)

To my wife Jenn, Sissy, Joe, Jaws, and Jellie to whom I owe a debt that can never be paid. To my fellow inmates for their inspiration and support in my darkest days.

Table of Contents

Sapere Aude

CHAPTER ONE
The Bin 101

It was approaching lunch time at the Pines, derisively referred to as the "Bin" by the mental patients held hostage at the institution. The inmates massed into the day room, reminiscent of circus clowns stuffing a tiny car to the gratuitous glee of the audience. It was an inexplicable Pine's ritual; the anticipation, the elation of any a small, nonviolent affair to break the monotony of the Bin, including a banal meal in the repurposed gym. Covid protocols be damned. Crazy people and politicians aren't subject to government mandates, viral infections, or ethical standards. It's science, and only a heretic would dare quarrel with science at mortal risk of facing the modern-day pyre of cancelation.

Trash bins were banned on the wards for ambiguous motives. Speculation ran the gamut from the trash receptacles' potential utilization as a clumsy weapon to their utility as a food source for the truly batshit crazy among the inmates, of which there were many. The floor and, curiously, the water fountain, were consequently littered with debris and food waste. One problem solved, yet another manifested. Unintended consequences are rarely factored into decision making, regardless of the mountain of "data" applied. The ward was understaffed with defeated, indifferent, at best and, at worst, sadistic employees; some of whom were easily better suited as inmates. Power over others attracts amateur psychopaths. The day room chairs were massed together with military precision, yet never cleaned. None of the patients, and only few of the staff half-heartedly wore masks that served to protect their chins from Covid infection.

The duty shrink called for Dakota. She was cowered in a corner and couldn't hear him over the din of the day room chatter. China was the self-declared "African Queen" of the ward. She held court and no one deigned to challenge the 300-pound, yet remarkably agile, woman. China was intelligent, charming, gracious, and amusing most of the time but could shift to feral predator in a blink of an eye on even the faintest of imagined affronts. She located Dakota in the corner and weighed through the crowd to escort her to the shrink. Missing "sessions" earned demerits. Enough demerits brought on an excuse to hold inmates extra days in captivity and, as such, were dispensed like candy by a drunken Shriner driving a go-cart at a St. Patrick's Day parade. Extra days were billable hours. Billable hours were bank to the Bin. Even if those missed sessions were the result of administered medications. Or falling on a wet floor and having to wait to be found and brought to a nurse for clearance to attend one's session. Billable hours was taught for the entire first hour at the Bin's new employee training session to all levels of staff. Everyone had a part to play to maximize profits. Patient care and safety was tertiary, and, even so, it was like watching a five-year-old quoting Shakespeare knuckle deep in his nose. Them the words, but…

China grabbed Jason's flat ass as she passed by. Without ample butt to hold up his jeans, he used tie wraps to cinch them around his waist. Necessity truly is the mother of invention. Belts, like kindness and quality patient care, were contraband on the ward. Jason whipped around with his fist drawn in preparation to strike but thoughtfully recoiled as he recognized a target of superior strength, agility, and insanity. "Go ahead, honey. China likes it rough. You, scraggy cracker, I'm gonna ride you like a cowboy and smother you with my magnificent, Nubian breasts." China fondled her breasts like a porn star wannabe on an Only Fans site. Jason silently turned away. "Don't walk away, boy. I smuggled some condoms up here in my prison purse. This here ain't my first rodeo. I gonna make you my prison bitch but I don't want none your scrawny ass retarded young 'uns. I got me seven deadbeats living at my mama's and my auntie's already. Next ones I gonna have gonna support their mama like the good Lord intended. Sure as shit can't depend on that orange mother fucker to do shit to care for me. But you, honey…I just gonna hate-fuck your redneck, racist ass 'til you wish you were dead." She moved on and fixated on Jack. "Now you, green eyes…I gonna have your babies. Old man like you probably can't last a damn minute in the sack, even if you can get it up. But Jason gonna take care of China's erotic needs. I just need some of your baby juice."

Jack smiled. "Nothing would give me more pleasure than to help bring a child into the world with you,

China. But I fear that is an impossible task." Jack was a pragmatist. Don't engage in a fight you can't win. Words are not like grenades, but carefully selected ones might often avoid said grenades.

"What, you got ED, cotton top? I'll get that tiny cracker dick up long enough to get your man seed." She licked a long, bedazzled nail.

Jack stifled his gag reflex as his sphincter tightened out of reflex. "I have little doubt a woman of your beauty and passions could manage. It's just that I'm shooting blanks, China." Jack made a snipping motion with his fingers as he was pondering the requisite calculus of the sexual act with such a large woman. "Now Wheels over there, he's smart as a whip and with a functioning baby maker."

"I don't want 'em just smart," she replied, despondently. "I want 'em pretty, cotton top. And not fucking angry all the time. Wheel's is ugly on the outside and the inside. And all those meds he on probably make a three-arm baby. Ain't nobody got no time for that, no matter how much disability bonus I'd get for that young 'un."

Wheels was offended. "Fuck your fat, heroin junkie ass," he slurred. China had made no secret of her Pine's origin story.

China smiled and latched on to Wheel's crotch with her bright talons. "Don't you wish, you pitiful little cripple boy? Play them cards right, though, and I let you give me a ride on your four-wheel stallion. That tiny little thing even work?" China genuinely inquired.

Jack sat quietly as he pondered the even more demanding physics of the act between the 300-pound China and 90-pound Derrick in a wheelchair with a 250-pound load limit before realizing he was burning images in his brain he might regret. Well, almost quietly.

A long, thick, whispery cloud emitted from Jack as his sphincter slowly relaxed at the realization China's attentions were now on Wheels. Jack made a mental note to check his drawers. Sharting is a disagreeable side effect of growing old.

This was the Bin. The rules of logic and polite society did not apply within these desecrated halls of healing. Wheels powerfully rammed his wheelchair into China's legs, knocking her to the ground. Half the inmates tumbled to the tile floor with her. "Damn...8,10 split," Wheels slurred and maniacally laughed. China rolled over, trying to stand before Wheels rammed into her again, knocking the remaining "pins" to the floor. His laugh pierced the ward like fingernails on a chalkboard. "And Wheels picks up the split for a spare." He awkwardly self high fived.

The Bin didn't employ security on ward three. The ward was where they housed the low risk, nonviolent patients. In reality, security cut into The Pines' profit margin and the security employees had unionized the previous year, thus raising the cost of labor. Profit margins first. Safety third. Half the inmates in the ward were on probation or were ex-convicts. In all fairness, they consisted mostly of nonviolent drug convictions... mostly. General mayhem ensued as Wheels continued to get the best of China, smartly not allowing her to regain her footing. In her frenzied struggles, she went about knocking others forcefully around. Dakota's head was bashed against a chair, rendering her unconscious while bleeding profusely. The tile floor was slick with blood and other best left anonymous fluids, subsequently suspending the food and trash debris among the inadvertent combatants in a thin layer of repugnant gruel. Shortly, everyone but Wheels was prone, writhing amongst the floating muck, clumsily attempting to purchase footing. Aides, an ironic title, from the other wards joined the chaos. They shouted in whispered tones (so as not to overtake the audio recording on their personal devices) for China and Wheels to stop from the safety of the perimeter. The aides were not so covertly enjoying the shitshow while judiciously avoiding the ever-growing pool of infectious gruel, doing nothing to assist their mentally-challenged charges. Situation normal. Clickbait acquired. Eventually China laid still, spent from the effort. Wheels, unprompted, rolled back to his room, sated in his day room triumph. China reached out and grabbed Jason's leg as he walked by, dragging him down to the floor. "I still gonna fuck your bitch ass to death."

At some point, all the inmates made way back to their rooms without assistance from the staff for "lock down". An ambulance was called for Dakota. In the chaos of the moment, China secreted into Jason's room. Jason, to his credit, put up a valiant fight, but the nonnegotiable laws of physics worked against him. China's vigor freed the bed from its floor bolts, slamming the bed into the wall with the unmistakable rhythmic motion of enthusiastic human copulation. Jason's muffled screams could scarcely be heard against the loud, feral moans of China, the dreadful shrieks of Jason's horrified roommate, and the cadenced thudding of the bed. The roommate should be judged lightly for his inaction, as he was without the requisite courage, wit, and industrial hydraulic tools to successfully intervene. Spent, China fell asleep atop Jason, who lay silently sobbing between gasps for air from between truly massive breasts, and pleas for a merciful bullet. The condom was no match for their violent, sexual hate-making. Nine months later, China would deliver her eighth child.

Jason filed a rape complaint with the staff, but his now catatonic roommate was unable to substantiate the complaint. China filed a counterclaim that Jason was the aggressor. The Pines reluctantly passed the complaints on to the police who wanted no part in the circus and filed just a cursory report regarding an alleged assault of sexual nature without witnesses or suitable evidence. Jason's outraged cougar girlfriend, Karen, hired an expensive lawyer and, in combination with her more carnal talents, convinced the district attorney to charge China. Months later, China's GoFundMe lawyer packed the courtroom with women wearing #MeToo t-shirts and, with the support of BLM activists, began a viral social media campaign. The middle-aged, white, male judge, ignoring the laws of physics, ruled China innocent in order to avoid the indignity of the mob's outrage. China filed a civil complaint and the judge ordered Jason, who had $132.10 in total assets and a tenth-grade education, to pay $5,000 in damages, $600 a month in child support for 18 years, and to set aside $10,000 for college tuition. Justice is blind…and unlike physics, negotiable.

Karen cut her losses and threw Jason to the curb. He was last seen in Bangkok working as a lady boy, supporting his perfectly healthy, yet somewhat dullard, daughter, Malaysia, and her mother, China. China reportedly bragged she had a good ride to get a good ride. "Didn't need me some lame old ass limp dick after all."

This world's justice is indeed blind. Some might add deaf, dumb, and fearful of the mob.

CHAPTER TWO
China

Days earlier…

A 911 call came into the emergency center from Zombieville, a collection of disheveled trailer parks situated on the lowest ring of hell for Marion County's considerable drug-addled populace. Zombieville was located adjacent to Highway 441, between Ocala and the Villages. The Villages were infamous for being a semi-spring break locale for the over-55, pre-dementia, and the multidose of curses that accompany the aging crowd. Known for its high rate of STDs, it was sort of a last gasp bachelor/bachelorette party before being warehoused in anticipation for the long, dark sleep. Marion County, on the other hand, is the epitome of old Florida; pre-Walt and the plague of obscene parks of adult torment and unsustainable credit card debt. Now, more than a bit worn around the edges, the community was once a trendy vacation destination and included attractions like Silver Springs with its nature tours in glass bottom boats and evening outdoor concerts, and Silver Dollar City offering a glimpse of the Wild West that never was in Central Florida. Then again, one should seldom let the truth get in the way of a good story. Especially when Yankee tourists' dollars were involved.

"Marion County Emergency Center," the seasoned dispatcher answered emotionlessly, as if the call was a request for the latest Beyonce song at the local radio station. Zombieland calls were predictable and annoying. The caller remained mute. This was not uncommon, given the number of opiate overdoses in the county. "What is the nature of your emergency," the dispatcher further probed.

After a protracted delay, whilst the dispatcher continued polishing her bedazzled nails, the caller grudgingly responded. "There's a fat black lady passed out on the kitchen floor blocking the refrigerator and, consequently, my access to cold beer." The caller sounded surprisingly lucid.

Marion County is home to some of the most beautiful horse farms and most expensive thoroughbreds in the world. This was not that. It is also home to the largest density of meth and crack producers and consumers in Florida. Zombieland was more that. Heaven and hell were equally represented in Marion County.

"Please provide the location of your emergency, sir," the dispatcher calmly requested. Emergency services had tapped out on geocoding Zombieland.

"Who you calling sir? I didn't tell you my preferred pronoun!" Portions of the woke culture had penetrated deep into society.

"Sorry, purple penguin. What is your preferred pronoun?"

"You can call me sir. Although I prefer Your Majesty," the caller mused, scratching his week-long growth. Small portions of woke in small helpings.

"Okay, sir. What is the nature of your emergency?"

"I done told you, lady. The fat, black bitch is blocking the darn refrigerator on the kitchen floor, and I want a beer." It was 9 am. Very small helpings.

"Sir, could we refrain from the profanity and stick to the facts."

"Ma'am, dem are the facts. It's not profanity. She self identifies as fat. A fat bitch is blocking my damn…I mean darn refrigerator and I need a fuc…frigging beer." The caller remembered his woke training at his day labor job site, allowing him to get on with the call.

The caller proceeded to kick the offending lady in the vicinity of her ribs, hoping to rouse her from her deep slumber, but to no avail. China, said offending lady, had snorted pure heroin, pinched from the Alabama Chapter of the Outlaws motorcycle club. The club had stopped at a local bar, Foul Balls, to park and swap out their trucks for their trailered bikes for the last leg of their journey to Daytona. It was the 80th anniversary of Bike Week and, despite Covid, the show must go on. Floridians pride themselves in freedom, thongs, sunshine, beaches, retention ponds, meth, and citrus fruits. The heroin was pure for ease of transportation on motorcycles and unguarded, 'cause, well, they were the Outlaws. No right-minded criminal would steal from them. Horace, the yet unnamed caller, was not much of a criminal and, on his best day, not remotely right-minded. And the last couple pure heroin days were not his best days. To be perfectly honest, they were also not his worst.

"Sir, I'm gonna need a street address and trailer number if you want that beer anytime soon." The dispatcher spoke fluent meth head. Normally the 911 system displayed a street address, but many of the trailer parks in Zombieland were a bit transitional in nature and, without specific addresses, windows, viable sewer systems, or registered occupants. Covid eviction restriction had further muddled up in semblance of order and, consequently, maintenance in the parks. The mail he/she/they had resorted to depositing the mail for the park in the unused recycling container at the park's entrance for the park's residents to sort the Bed, Bath and Beyond coupons, mail-order brides seeking a better life anywhere in the US of A, and debt collections letters for themselves. Electric and water service was currently available only due to Covid non-pay disconnection restrictions and creative engineering from turned power linemen on the occasional lucid day.

"Just how the hell should I know, lady?" Horace questioned the dispatcher. "This dump ain't my domicile of record...I got curtains on my windows with little Mickey and Minnie Mice fornicating in various positions of the Kama Sutra. Hee, Hee...," Horace snorted at his creative wit and continued, "... and I'm high as a mother-fucking vulture combing the ground for fresh roadkill on a hot, summer day on I-4 in downtown Orlando at rush hour."

The veteran dispatcher had already sent police and rescue units to the general vicinity of the call. Not her first circus, not her first clown. "Lovely visual, sir. I'll be sure to claw my eyes out after my shift. Can you please open the door and listen for sirens and direct the emergency units to your location? And may I have your name, sir?"

"First off, Lucille...May I call you Lucille? You sound like my last lady friend. She had a nice smile 'fore she went and lost 'em. I try and warn her about that damn meth." He sobbed for a moment while pondering his lost, toothless love and irrationally fantasizing about future possibilities with the unnamed dispatcher. The dispatcher scoffed and screwed the top back on her nail polish. "Secondly, Lucille, they ain't no Goddamn door on this here trailer, and finally, I don't need no emergency vehicles. What I be needing me here is a damn crane. You know, like they build them tall-ass, see-through buildings in Orlando. I need to move this fat bitch away from the damn refrigerator. You just like Lucille...you don't listen to me. You still got your teeth?" His voice rose hopefully with each syllable. Horace set the bar low, but a toothless smile was a nonstarter and a rather a common issue in the crowd in which he ran. Horace, despite his own considerable shortcomings, had standards. In his mind's eye, he was still the relatively handsome man before drugs had ravaged his body, mind, and soul.

"Your name, sir?" The dispatcher persisted in her endeavor to stick to her script.

"I'll show you mine if you will show me yours first."

"Sir, this is not an Only Fans site. It's a 911 emergency center, and I need your name, please."

"Yours first."

"Okay, sir, then its Lucille," the dispatcher conceded, tossing her script to the side.

"Damn, I knew it. Its Horace, darlin'. I've missed you so. Did you get your teeth fixed?"

The Dispatcher heard the sirens grow in volume through the phone and relayed the target address was nearby and without a door. The drivers quickly spotted the ramshackle trailer and pulled into the yard, which was littered with beer cans, car parts, empty packages of Sudafed, cigarette butts, and human and animal feces.

Some of the lucid kids in the neighborhood would toss bite-sized candy on the ground, creating a fun game called chocolate or poo for lawn stragglers in their meth stupor.

As a matter of course, the cops responded with EMTs to Zombieland. Truth be told, a platoon of the National Guard in hazmat suits also should be dispatched to every call. The cops entered first, cuffed Horace, and cleared a spot for him on the soiled, shag carpeted, living room floor. After a cursory sweep of the trailer for covertly armed Zombies, the cops waved the EMTs in. The EMTs went to work on the fat lady blocking the fridge.

"Damn, dude. That pinches. Can you grab me a beer once you move the fat lady? Please?" Horace politely asked. "I ain't had my breakfast and my blood sugar is low." Always try honey first, his mom had taught him. Then get the bat. Mom was a good Christian lady who brought Horace up in the ways of the Old Testament fire and brimstone God between lockups, rehabs, and Baker Acts.

"Ma'am, what drugs have you taken?" calmly inquired the EMT while trying to penetrate the fog of the lady's drug-induced coma. The lady clutched a crack pipe in one hand and a lighter in the other. She did not respond, but she was breathing and had a weak but steady pulse. While the two EMTs worked out the physics of lifting and transporting her down the steep, rickety stairs to the ambulance (in sum, the EMTs weighed less than half of her), the cops continued questioning Horace to little effect.

"Shit, man. For the love of baby Jesus, can you get that fat lady away from the refrigerator?" or some derivative was Horace's only response to any question posed to him.

The rookie cop, still naive in the ways of Marion County's drug underbelly, surveyed the room for signs of illegal activity. The veteran did not. He knew damn well it was there and was satisfied with blissful ignorance. Every trailer in this park likely either manufactured, stored, or sold illegal substances. Too much paperwork. "Yo, Jesus." Emmitt tried to focus Jesus away from any possible evidence of illegal activity.

"Check this out, jefe," the rookie cop said excitedly.

Emmitt, the veteran, responded. "What the hell, man, we've talked about this..." He stopped mid-sentence. Jesus held up a 50-gallon, black garbage bag full of dozens of smaller bags. One bag was sliced open and contained what appeared to be heroin.

Horace cocked a suspicious eye at Jesus. "Imposter! Everybody know Jesus is a white man and he don't steal or lie or none of that bad shit. That bag is mine. Just put it back down and get that fat black lady the hell away from the refrigerator!" Horace calculated the situation had escalated and it was now time for the bat. Perhaps "woke" had not trickled down to Horace's particular level of hell at all.

Meanwhile, the EMTs were beginning to execute their nascent plan to transport the fat lady. Step one was to remove the crack pipe and lighter from her hands. No small feat that, as she clutched them both tightly, like a rabid dog with a fresh, meaty bone. The older EMT used a pair of pliers to pry the lighter from her vise-like grip, briefly waking her from her slumber. She did not release the lighter, but instead flicked it to light the pipe in the other hand.

"Ma'am. Stop that!" She feebly kicked at them in response and continued to light the pipe. The EMTs surrendered to the inevitable.

"What's your name, Ma'am?"

She cracked a suspicious eye. "What your name, you tiny-dicked, white devil? What is this, a KKK convention of short crackers? Leave me the hell alone 'fore I call Reverend Farrakhan. Give me my damn cell. I got that righteous mother fucker on speed dial for occasions like this, surrounded by a herd of short-ass racists in matching khaki britches." She took a long drag on the pipe and laid her head back down.

She cracked one eye and took another drag from the pipe. "Your mama still dress you?"

"Your name, Ma'am?"

"Jesus Christ, you persistent little Bobbsey Twins. China," she responded. "That's my name. Now go fuck yourself or each other as you see fit. China don't judge."

The senior EMT corrected China's reference. "They were fraternal twins, the Bobbseys...a boy and a girl."

The junior EMT shrugged his shoulders. "What the hell you even talking about?"

Jesus tagged and deposited the plastic bag of drugs into the trunk of the police cruiser. Emmitt consulted with the EMTs on best practices to safely extricate China from the trailer. "Best solution is if we can get her up to walk. The door is too narrow for your gurney, and I don't think the steps can take the weight." The EMT's nodded in agreement. "You got something you can give her to wake her up enough to walk?" Emmitt asked the EMTs.

"Nothing legal," the junior EMT shrugged his shoulders.

"The four of us can drag her to the door and we can just give her a little nudge from there. Let gravity do her thing," Jesus offered. He used hand gestures to artfully illustrate his point.

"Let's put a pin in that," Emmitt replied. They all stood in a semi-circle around the subject, peering down perplexed, each secretly considering the Jesus solution, although certain it was not listed as an option in the best practice's manual. "Can you get your backboard in here? We can position the board underneath her and slide her out the door and down the stairs." Emmitt, unlike Jesus, made a series of befuddling motions with his hands to illustrate his plan like a traveling Missionary Baptist choir leader, sans any musical training, leading the congregation under the canvas in a spirited, off-key hymnal whilst the collection plate hungrily circulated through the worshipers and the snakes angrily hissed and rattled in their cages.

China briefly roused and squinted at the men. "What the hell, you ugly-ass crackers looking at?"

Jesus took offense. "I ain't no cracker!"

China apologized. "Sorry, my brother," she slurred. "Now get your smelly, beaner ass away from me."

"Less offended now, Jesus?" Emmitt sarcastically inquired.

Horace interjected from the adjacent room. "I'll shoot the bitch for you if that'll get me a beer any damn faster."

"No thanks, Horace. You just sit quietly over yonder and ponder the error of your ways," Emmitt nonchalantly replied.

"Can we just put a pin in Horace's offer, as well? It has certain merits worth considering," suggested Jesus.

Emmitt shook his head, already dreading the paperwork load just for the captain to claim the credit for such a large bust.

The junior EMT returned with the backboard, and, with considerable effort, half the team lifted her dead weight while the other half situated the board underneath. The straps unfortunately were of insignificant breadth to secure her onto the board, except across her knees. In hindsight, the team discovered this was a critical, tactical error in their plan. Math is hard. Physics even more so. The four-man team lifted her by setting the bottom of the board onto the first step where the board's edge firmly secreted into a crack in the steps. The EMTs lifted the top of the board at a dangerously steep angle in an effort to initiate the gravitational pull requisite to theoretically slide the board, with China, down the steps. Regrettably, the laws of physics engaged in an unforeseen fashion, tipping China's unsecured top half over her secured bottom half, causing her to face plant into the debris-filled yard, like a "wrong" whale carcass tossed unceremoniously from a Japanese whaler.

"Guess we took that pin out, Emmitt," Jesus responded.

Emmitt rolled his eyes. The four managed to load her onto the ambulance and it raced away to Orlando Memorial emergency room where, after a cursory diagnosis and patch job, she was transported to the Bin.

Emmitt moved Horace's handcuffs to the front and handed him a cold Natty out of the fridge before securing him in the backseat of the cruiser and tossing a second beer into the back within his reach. Emmitt felt Horace was in for a long period of forced sobriety, only to be followed by a series of subsequent benders interrupted by the occasional incarceration. Emmitt knew you can't help someone who does not want help. He did what he could, but this was not his first experience with addicts.

Jesus cocked his head and said, "I don't think that is protocol".

"And throwing China down the stairs was?" Emmitt retorted. "Your parents named you poorly. Let's at least try being a bit human."

Jesus shrugged his shoulders. "They were more Old Testament fire and brimstone Catholics than the love and forgiveness type."

"Maybe they should have named you Cain."

The radio crackled to life. "All units, all units. Respond to the 3000 block of Blitchton Road and be on the lookout for a white male, 5'8", and 95 pounds. He is to be considered armed and dangerous." The dispatcher seemed more frantic than normal. Emmitt looked in the rearview mirror to see Horace had finished his first beer and was peacefully napping.

"Let's ride," Jesus said, excited to do some real police work not involving junkies, prostitutes, domestic violence, or some permutation thereof.

Emmitt silently debated the correct course of action, knowing he should procedurally return to the station with Horace and the drugs, but genuinely concerned about leaving the sparse Ocala police officers without backup. Police officers are a close-knit brotherhood. And from his experience, small men were the most dangerous. They suffered from Napoleonic complex and needed to conquer the world to prove they had a big dick. He chose, "Let's ride", and flipped on the cruiser's lights and siren to Jesus' childlike delight.

Shortly, the two observed the circling helicopters and assumed the treacherous fugitive was likely nearby. They raced down a twisting, live oak tree canopied, dirt road to a barn.

CHAPTER THREE

Jason

Helicopters buzzed treacherously low over a wooded area of the county adjacent to a horse farm. A pack of bloodhounds were released, swarming the wooded area with ominous fervor. Dozens of police cars, sirens a-blazing, combed the narrow, back roads. The SWAT team arrived, theatrically bailing out of their armored vehicle as if storming the beaches of Normandy, using crisp hand signals to deftly deploy into the woods in a choreographed formation. Million-dollar thoroughbreds strained against fetters or nervously sprinted about the luscious, green, rolling hills, eyeballing the wooden fence enclosures for escape routes whilst silently performing the requisite calculus to obtain the necessary escape velocity vital to clear the whitewashed fences. The owner of the farm, a large GOP political contributor, was on the phone with the

Governor, yelling creative permutations of obscenities. Jason was in the barn mucking shit and listening to death metal music from the '80's at full volume on his knock-off Air Pods.

The Governor dutifully conferenced in the State Attorney General, who conferenced in the local district attorney, who in turn conferenced in three sheriffs from nearby counties. The age-old game of political "cover-your-ass" had been initiated. Shit doth run downhill. There would be a sacrificial lamb for any screw-ups, likely some low-level employee who had nothing to do with creating the situation. Florida was turning purple due to the influx of damn Yankees ignoring the climate change religion they embraced, migrating to the state for its low taxes, liberties, low violent crime rates, beautiful beaches and warm weather but bringing with them the very liberal politics that created the conditions they were escaping. Hence the difference between a Yankee and a damn Yankee. A Yankee comes to visit; a damn Yankee stays. Marion County and its wealthy horse ranches were now, more than ever, paramount in keeping the state red and the Governor in the state house with his lovely bride who enjoyed the finer things in life that the Governor himself was not amongst.

"What in gawd's name are you fools doing? You damn sure best have a serial killer on the loose after dining on the Governor's pretty little wife," exclaimed the horse farmer, picturing the Governor's wife's tight ass. The farmer had a bit of a crush on the Governor's wife and had gamed out scenarios on taking the Governor's job and his wife as his trophy bride without upsetting the large evangelical electorate. The Governor took charge. "Which one of you imbeciles is responsible for this here circus and what in gawd's name is happening?" He spoke with an overbaked, Southern accent. He was a

Harvard grad, born in the Northeast with a silver spoon in his mouth, and had made daddy proud by adding to the family fortune by peddling legal drugs illicitly and through a series of effective Medicare fraud schemes. He now continued to enrich his cronies and himself from within the hallowed halls of the statehouse. The Governor was charming, brilliant, without morals, greedy, power hungry and fearless. The most treacherous brand of politician.

There was a brief moment of silence on the phone. Standard protocol would have the next imbecile in line grab the ball, but the Attorney General secured his position on his good looks, college football career, purported faith in the good Lord, picture perfect family, and charm...not his political savvy and certainly not his concussion-addled IQ. The Attorney General finally broke the silence, likely prompted by his ever-present aide. Some intimated the aide slept on a cot next to the AG and confiscated his phone during bathroom and rare conjugal visits. Others scoffed at the suggestion the aide ever left his side and, perhaps, assisted the AG with all of his activities. "Did Tiger get lost in the woods?" asked the Attorney General. Tiger Woods was considered a Florida treasure and his loss would warrant such a massive response. The aide had already dialed the General for the National Guard in preparation for activation should Tiger prove to be in the wild or under attack by a Scandinavian woman yielding a seven iron after having just survived an automobile accident with a tree.

The Marion County Sheriff spoke up. "No, sir. I believe Tiger is in the hospital with a broken leg in California. Sirs...we are searching for one Jason Born."

"You gotta be fucking kidding me," the horse farmer responded.

"No, sir. That is the suspect's name."

"No, you damn fool, I know him. The little bastard is in my barn mucking shit as we speak. Call off your gawd damn search before I sue the short britches right off your scrawny, redneck asses. What the hell you want that good for nothing bastard for: jay-walking while stupid, eating boogers within 100 yards of a school, picking his Wranglers out the crack of his scrawny ass in public, pissing into the wind, howling at the moon in broad daylight, failure to recycle a beer can, or farting in church?"

Nobody deigned to respond to the farmer's outburst.

The farmer broke the silence. "That little bastard damn well had ran Tiger through with a pitchfork at TPC and, even then, you nitwits ever thought to check Jason's place of employment before calling in the Calvary?"

"Marchman Acted," the Sheriff mumbled while shuffling through the jacket his ever-present assistant handed him.

"Marmalade Acted! For the love of all things holy. What the hell is that? He poke his wiener in a jar of marmalade during the Saint Patrick's Day Parade dressed as a Leprechaun, run buck-ass nakid through Publix covered in marmalade, scoop a glob of marmalade on a bike trail and watch the riders pile up in the slippery goo, cover his dick in marmalade and have your mama lick it off?"

The Attorney General bravely interrupted the farmer's tirade and corrected him. "Marchman Acted, sir. He has been committed to the Bi…The Pines Mental Hospital."

"I don't give a rats what you call it. What did he do to warrant deploying Seal Team Six, the Blue Angels, the Calvary, the Mounties, the Rangers, the Proud Boys,

Dawg the Bounty Hunter, and a pack of blood hounds to search for him?" Dawg was not to be confused with the well-known bounty hunter by a similar sounding name. This Dawg was a knock-off version who had a buzzcut but wore a purchased mullet when in public for effect. He hung out at tourist locations, posed for pictures, and groped middle-aged women's asses with alarming impunity. He also won the Masters. "Don't judge a book..." and all.

"Says here...," the Sheriff leafed through his file, "... domestic violence while under the use of narcotics."

"You ignorant bastard. His girlfriend outweighs him by 50 pounds. She is deader than a doornail."

"No, sir. I believe she is at the nail spa." The Sheriff was familiar with Jason's girlfriend.

A police car, sirens blaring, arrived at the barn and came to a sliding halt, propelling a wall of dust and gravel over the farmer. It was the final straw. He lifted a Glock from his shoulder holster and carelessly emptied it into the police car, nicking Emmitt in the thigh and spraying shards of glass across Jesus' forehead and hands. Fortunately, none were seriously injured but the car was toast.

When the dust settled, Jesus exited the bullet-ridden car with his arms extended, bleeding from his side, forehead, and hands. The farmer exclaimed, "Jesus Christ," in response to Jesus' inadvertent stigmata.

Several hours later, Horace woke unharmed but confused after having been towed to the police impound lot while still locked in the back of the now disabled cruiser. He howled and banged on the window to no effect other than finding the second beer. Horace drank the beer in a couple of gulps and settled back in for a nap. In the carnage, both Emmitt and Jesus had overlooked both the drugs and Horace.

CHAPTER FOUR

Gaia

There is a gathering of derelict biker bars and biker wannabe bars on Highway 40 heading east out toward Ormond Beach from Ocala. The bars are frequented by a volatile mix of meth heads, small time hoodlums, accidental tourists, and the occasional real deal biker, the one percenters: The Outlaws, Hells Angels, Mongrels...

Foul Balls was a staple on the strip and popular with the bikers. Every night was lady's night at the bar with management's fervent desire to increase the female to male ratio and lessen the violence over fighting for the attention of the sparse serviceable pickings that dared the perilous surroundings. The drinks were watered down for profit and safety purposes, but even yet, a determined drinker, combined with illicit, readily available substances, could get snockered. Fights were a common theme over women, pool, insults (both real and imagined), and, occasionally, colors. For those of you not versed in biker jargon, colors is the term used to identify members of clubs and locations. The One-Percenter's don't play when it comes to colors. It was the reason souvenir t-shirts from bike week were offered in a limited selection. Gun fights were uncommon but not unheard of. Beatings with less deadly weapons by tacit mutual consent only befell on days ending in "y".

The familiar sound of a pool cue snapping pierced the background noise of the bar. The bartender, Earl, a ubiquitous fixture of the bar, speed-dialed 9 on his cell phone, laid it on the bar, grabbed a monogrammed Louisville Slugger named MR. T, and headed to the back to help the bar's solitary bouncer, who was deep into a handle of Jack devoid of a single drop of Jack. Earl mumbled about his lack of pay but, realistically, a rap sheet more than a dozen pages was a decided detriment to typical employment opportunities.

"Goddamn it, Gaia! What now?" Earl pleaded. The bar had a restraining order on Gaia, but none was foolish enough to attempt to enforce it without being in possession of automatic weapons. Not to infer automatic weapons were not present at any given time. Gaia was one of those women who could be pretty, but she chose not to be. As is, she was of average build and more of the handsome sort with dark eyes that were both captivating and frightening. The Outlaws offered her a position as "house mouse" for their club but she declined, advising she was "nobody's bitch". Normally, said offer was a formality, more a directive than an invitation. But Gaia was anything but normal and the Outlaws respected her "balls".

Earl entreated Gaia to put her weapon down. Instead, she swung the broken cue stick violently in the direction of a pudgy, middle-aged man who was likely an accidental tourist searching for a bit of adventure and respite from his family's enchanted vacation suffering two-hour lines in the summer sun for a 45-second magical adventure. "What is it, Gaia?" Earl asked.

Gaia responded with a feral grunt and another lunge toward her target, coming dangerously close to improving, or, at least, rearranging, a rather bulbous, sunburnt nose. "He touch you?" Earl asked. Gaia lunged. "He insult you?" Gaia lunged. "He cheat?" Gaia lunged and connected squarely against the man's ribcage. The tourist shrieked. The sound of sirens grew louder in the bar. Earl just needed to buy some time to keep the man alive. Not that Earl gave a damn about the man, but Foul Balls was short-listed by the city to be closed due to chronic violent crime, and, frankly, Earl needed the job.

"How much was the bet, $20? I'll take it off your tab." Women drank free in the bar and the bar did not run tabs. Gaia took a swing at Earl for insulting her intelligence but missed. "Okay, okay, cash, then." Gaia eyed him suspiciously before connecting with another swing on the man now lying in a puddle of his own pee on the floor that was pre-soaked with decades of spilt beer, blood, puke, sweat, tobacco juice, and multigenerational piss. Hygiene was nowhere to be found on the bar's list of priorities. There was the requisite mask sign on the door but was universally ignored as was the no fire arms, and obligatory no shirt, no shoes, no service sign. Foul Balls was as close as the genuine Wild West experience anywhere in Florida had to offer.

Emmitt and Jesus, fresh from a quick patch job at the ER, screeched to a halt outside the bar in the decommissioned morgue van, their patrol car now on the injured reserve list. The blood-stained officers jostled their way through the crowd to the back of the bar, each patron steadfastly vying for the best spot to record a video for their Insta account. No matter how poor or hungry one's children might be, cell phones and crack pipes were standard gear. One found money for the necessities in life. Emmitt spotted Gaia first. "Will this weekend never end," he mumbled to no one in particular. Police work in Marion County was like babysitting a family of toddlers who were outfitted with guns, knives, and drugs instead of books, balls, and puzzles.

Jesus charged into the fray and was greeted by a smack in the vest with the cue stick. Gaia took the opportunity to hit the accidental tourist again. The tourist flinched and grunted. "Slow your roll, Jesus. You leveled up with this one." Emmitt turned to the rookie. "Jesus, try and move the crowd back a bit." Jesus began to bleed from his forehead and palms again as he waved the crowd back with outstretched arms. The once avid Baptist crowd complied, some mistakenly crossing themselves, forgetting their religious origins. Mama had brought 'em up right, but poverty and drugs were more powerful than even a good upbringing and the words written in red. Emmitt turned to Gaia. "Can we not kill the poor bastard? How much he owe you?"

Gaia finally answered. "Five dollars, but he disrespected me and has to pay punitive damages."

"How much then Gaia, $20?" Whack. "50?" Whack. "Okay, $100?"

Gaia started to swing but stopped. "Cash?"

"You got $100, mister?" Emmitt asked the tourist.

"Fuck that crazy bitch. Arrest her." Whack, whack, whack.

"Slow down, Gaia. If you kill him, we got a whole lot of paperwork to do, and his kids will miss the teacups. Nobody wants that."

"It's fucking Harry Potter tomorrow." The Yankee tourist felt the need to correct Emmitt.

"Who's fucking Harry Potter tomorrow?" A bystander in the back who had no context to the comment due to being out of hearing range asked his buddy.

"I dunno, some Yankee dude."

An undercover reporter with a curiously large mustache who had fallen from grace was trying to get an exclusive on bike week to get some semblance of a career back. Upon overhearing this conversation, he quickly shifted gears. Within moments, the reporter had unleashed his clickbait as an exclusive report verified by an "anonymous" source he couldn't identify due to journalistic integrity that Harry Potter was not just an ally of the LGBTQ+69 but a member. This landed the reporter a recurring role as an anchor on a primetime show. After his mishaps in the 1980's, he was back.

"Oh, man. You are in for a long day of standing in line," Emmitt replied. "Maybe I should just let her put you in the hospital at least." The crowd murmured in agreement. "Gaia, don't you think that is equitable punishment? Besides, his wife is gonna give him another beating about being out late tonight."

Whack.

"I'll take that as a hard no."

Ever since George Floyd's murder by men not fit to wear a uniform and the resultant rise of the naïve Defund the Police movement, police have been reluctant to use force in any situation. Emmitt was by nature a kind man who abhorred violence to begin with. His service jacket held nothing but honors and was free from even a solitary citizen complaint.

"Earl, you got a $100 bill in the till?"

"Damn it, Emmitt. You know I'll get fired." Earl reluctantly made his way back to the cash register for the money.

Emmitt reached out toward Gaia. "Cash for the pool stick…deal?"

"And I get to walk out of here a free woman."

"Hold them horses, Gaia. That was not part of the deal. We have to get this man to the hospital and get him stitched up. We have to take you to the station to do a bit of paperwork. His wife is gonna want to see a police report to back his crazy-ass story."

"Eat my hairy cooter, Emmitt." Whack, whack, whack. Gaia tore off all her clothes and started swinging wildly at the crowd, connecting as frequently as not. Yet still, the patrons jockeyed for position to video the feral, naked woman indiscriminately whacking the bar patrons, cops, and the bleeding, accidental tourist who was still curled in the fetal position on the floor. Gaia was simultaneously yelling obscenities at volume levels like those of middle class, teenage, white boys trying to be gangster in cheap rides with sound systems worth more than their entire vehicle.

The inexplicable obsession with capturing video for Instagram cuts across all demographics and will eventually get someone killed. Both cops emptied their tasers into Gaia's naked flesh. Jesus reloaded and accidentally fired into Earl. Earl flopped on the floor like a saltwater catfish being introduced to land. Confused patrons rapidly swapped their cell phones from one scene to another, uncertain which chaotic panorama would acquire the most likes. Gaia, unfazed, dropped the stick and yanked the darts from her body. Emmitt seized the opportunity to bear hug Gaia, accidentally cupping his gloved hands directly over her bare breast.

The video of the sexual offending cop went viral. Later, Emmitt was fired for conduct unbecoming an officer and barely escaped prosecution for sexual assault. He and his family moved to Wyoming to escape the nightly protests and media blitz. New York's Governor Cuomo held a nationally televised press conference condemning the Florida Police Officer for his sex crimes and the Florida governor for not enforcing mask mandates. CNN, with its ratings in the tank, did not blur out Gaia's privates for purposes of "journalistic integrity". The bartender, Earl, was fired and found a job mucking horse shit that had ironically opened up that very same day.

CHAPTER FIVE

Wheels

Shady Grove Estates was in an upper-class, gated community just south of town. A wheelchair-bound young man with cerebral palsy finished off a fifth of Jack Daniels and angrily flung the bottle at the image of Donald J. Trump on his 60" television. His name was Derrick, but everyone who knew him called him Wheels. At least behind his back. Casual acquaintances and strangers typically stuck with calling him some colorful derivative of asshole. Wheels typically countered with some retort of at least he, as an asshole, was useful as opposed to the person calling him as such. He would continue to support his argument by refuting no one liked Socrates, either. Others agreed but countered Socrates was executed for pretty much being a quarrelsome asshole. Wheels' IQ was off the charts, and, like Socrates, he invited confrontational argument.

Wheels' birthfather hit the road when Wheels was eight. His mom was smoking hot and caught the pervy eye of her divorce attorney in spite of her baggage: a hot tempered, wildly intelligent, disabled son. The attorney failed to properly calculate the hot to crazy ratio but, to his credit, had stayed in the marriage. Wheels was prescribed a high dosage of Prozac and Zyprexa but rarely took the meds, as it dulled his cognitive "super" powers and his ability to feel emotion. Even if that primary emotion was rage.

It was minutes before midnight and the blessed end to their shift when Jesus and Emmitt were dispatched to the domestic disturbance call to Shady Grove. The stepfather had called it in from his oak-walled and marble floor study without bothering to even check on the commotion. This was not his first rodeo. Emmitt recognized the dispatched address and muttered "for the love of God," under his breath. Jesus subconsciously rubbed his forehead, spreading blood from brow to hairline.

Emmitt pulled the morgue van up to the community's gate. "Which old codger kicked it tonight?" the bored guard inquired.

"Just open the damn gate, Mutt." Emmitt's leg hurt and his wife had sent him a link of the Gaia video with a caption of "WTF, Emmitt". He was in no mood to satisfy the security guard's curiosity and boredom. Emmitt pulled under the home's elaborate portico, sans siren or flashing lights, and was greeted by Wheels' mother in lingerie unsuited for the occasion. She warmly embraced Emmitt, pressing her unfettered breast against his Kevlar vest. Emmitt was a frequent and favored visitor and consoler. Wheels' mom secretly coveted more. Emmitt, on the other hand, was a faithful husband and was clueless to her flirtations. Jesus covertly snapped a photo and posted it on Instagram. The photo went viral in conjunction with the Gaia image and #metoo, #timesup, and #defundthecops. A brave, anonymous keyboard warrior doxed Emmitt and, later that evening, he faced an angry mob of Beta males and Alpha women at his home, all wearing pink vagina hats and placards comparing Emmitt to bacon, Hitler, Epstein, and Trump.

"He off his meds?" Emmitt asked, knowing the answer.

Wheels' mom sobbed in response. Emmitt tenderly wiped a tear away. Jesus offered a hug to the three-quarter naked, despondent mom but was stiff-armed with a firm handshake. "Ew." She glanced at his bloody head. "Yeah," she said, turning her attention back to Emmitt. "His dad has already called the judge and had him Marchman Acted. I am afraid you're his ride to the Bin." The Bin was the derisive nickname of the local psychiatric hospital officially titled The Pines. It was not known for its standard of patient care but was, however, known widely for its lack of hygienic protocols. In fact, it was the abysmal patient care and unhygienic conditions that got it a starring role in a "what not to do" training video in the industry. The Bin marketed this on pamphlets as "setting industry standards", omitting the standards set were the low bar. Even Doctor Mengele had higher standards, if not worse outcomes.

Emmitt knocked lightly on Wheels' bedroom door. It was eerily silent. Jesus, always the impatient one, burst in and was greeted with a well-aimed and forcefully thrown crystal whiskey glass to his already bloodied forehead, subsequently knocking him to the ground. "You ever hear the phrase 'fools rush in', Jesus? Gonna get you crucified," Emmitt whispered.

"But I'll just take the weekend off and come back," Jesus sarcastically replied.

"You going straight to hell, Jesus."

"Not according to the book my Abuela read to me."

Emmitt scoffed and, from the safety of the hallway, helped Jesus to his feet. "Come on, Derrick. You know the drill. Let's make this easy on all of us."

Wheels cackled with manic laughter. "A bit late for that one." He threw another glass towards Jesus but only caught him in the vest.

"You little mother fu..." Jesus started to charge into the room, but Emmitt held him back.

"Trust me. You ain't that Jesus. You were born, you suffer, and you will die just like the rest of us. And, if you keep rushing in there like a damn fool, you gonna die today."

Wheels spent three hours a day in the gym. He was wasted away from the waist down, but his upper body was toned. He could bench press 300 pounds, almost three times his body weight. In his hands, the wheelchair was a lethal weapon unto itself. And there was no telling if he was otherwise armed. Beyond crystal whiskey glasses, of course.

"How we gonna play it tonight, Wheels? Resisting just gonna buy you more time in the Bin. Ain't nobody want that for you."

"Alright. Let's play a game. Riddle me this, Emmitt. What is time? Give me a suitable answer and I will come without a fight."

"Let's just tase the asshole and get home," Jesus suggested.

"You got a functioning taser on you, Jesus? I don't. Want to just shoot him?"

"I wouldn't rule it out," Jesus responded. Emmitt frowned. "I know...put a pin in it." Jesus unsnapped the holster for his service revolver should Emmitt have a change of heart.

"Okay, Wheels. I'll play. I know you're smarter than I am, but I got nothing to lose." Emmitt chose the shorter route to ending the call.

Wheels cackled. "You don't say. I expect that's a pretty low bar, but okay, Emmitt. Let's play a game. What is time?" His speech slurred from a combination of his malady and the whiskey.

Most learned observers might suggest something to the effect that time was the fourth dimension, a method of measuring the progress of existence. Lesser observers may refer to a clock, a meager, measurement tool typically off by near an hour half the year. Emmitt knew Wheels better. "Time...well it's just a silly conscript of man to measure something that is not measurable and perhaps doesn't even exist." Emmitt went to Ocala Junior College on the GI Bill after two tours in Iraq with the Marines. Don't mistake education with intelligence or toughness with compassion.

Wheels rolled out of the room down the hall and to the front door silently and up the ramp to the morgue van. A deranged grin crossed his face when he spotted the van. "The irony drips from the wealthy shyster's gilded portico like tears from heaven," he slurred as they drove off heading for The Pines.

CHAPTER SIX

Dakota

Forty miles or so west of Ocala lies the quaint, coastal, fishing village of Homosassa. The community sits on Highway 19, once known as the Dixie Highway prior to all things Southern, both the good and bad, being expunged from the history books. Napoleon suggested history was a pack of lies agreed upon. Others suggest he should have added and rewritten every decade or so by those who did not live it. More than a few haughty millennials could benefit from a history lesson on Sherman and his Total Warfare concept during his infamous march through Georgia and South Carolina. An honest examination might just help one understand some Southerner's views on the War of Northern Aggression. Be reminded, history is always penned by the victors and, as such, perhaps biased in their favor, omitting the victors' sins in the conflict while overstating the sins of the losers. After all, it is a very thin line between a patriot and a traitor: victory.

Central Florida, outside of Orlando proper, runs deep red. God, guns, trucks, and the American flag rule the hearts and minds of most. The concept of more than two sexes, abortion, or gun laws goes against their very moral fabric. Not judging. Just saying, not a great place for a young, transgender woman to come of age.

Dakota was a tiny, delicate flower who had just turned 21 years old. In appearance, she looked similar to Dorothy of Oz but her personality more befit the Cowardly Lion: timid and innocent. Left uninformed, most would never suspect she was a biological male. Her parents, and, even more so, her grandparents, struggled with Dakota's sexuality. Through middle school, she was taunted relentlessly as being a sissy. In high school, she came out and started dressing as a girl. The taunting grew worse, and, without a support system, she fell further into depression. Once she turned 18, she started a regiment of hormones and underwent gender reassignment surgery with the financial and moral assistance of a more enlightened aunt who had fled Central Florida to California. After returning to Florida, Dakota dyed her short locks red and worked as a mermaid at a local old Florida tourist attraction known as Weeki Wachee.

Dakota's parents never got totally on board with her new life, but they loved her and tried the best they knew how. But mom noticed behind the mask of innocence something seminal had changed in her daughter and not just the plumbing modification. Something darker. Dakota moved out and soon found a boyfriend who enjoyed her physical company but, like most 20-something-year-old boys, was not the supportive type, unless it involved tickling his johnson in some performative manor.

Dakota's boyfriend had yet to return home from a night out with the boys at three in the morning. He was ignoring her texts and calls. Some keyboard fundamentalist assholes had found her social media sites and were relentlessly bullying her online. WWJD and all. Irony and hypocrisy is lost on the extremes of both sides of the political equation. She tried to advocate for the young LGBTQ+ community in Central Florida, but really was not strong enough to handle the backlash from doing so. An encrypted message entered her timeline. She drank her fourth glass of rosé, swallowed the prescribed 11 Tylenol pills, and texted her mom, dad, and boyfriend she had consumed a bunch of pills in order to attempt to kill herself.

Dakota's dad saw the text when he got out of bed to pee early that same morning and called 911. Thank God for enlarged prostates. The EMTs found Dakota, still alone, sobbing, and throwing up into the toilet, and transferred her to the hospital in nearby Crystal River. The hospital faculty deemed her medically fit later that day and Baker Acted her to the Bin in Ocala.

CHAPTER SEVEN
Bank and the Outlaws

One day prior…

The advanced crew of the Alabama Outlaws pulled into the parking lot of Foul Balls in two F-150 extended cab pickups that were towing trailers packed with five Harleys, an Indian, and ten kilos of pure heroin. It was easier to transport the uncut drugs by bike. Amazon was transporting the cutting and packaging material straight to the safe house. God bless Jeff Bezos and his legion of knock-off, third-party sellers peddling shoplifted, defective, fell off a truck, and/or counterfeited items at discounted prices. After cutting the heroin, it had a street value of between a quarter- to half-million dollars. They pulled around back to the gravel parking lot. The Outlaws unloaded their bikes and went inside for a piss and a cold beer before they rode the final leg into Daytona. Apache said he needed a quick lay. Bank pointed him to a neighboring rub and tug and reminded him a cash tip was expected for a happy ending.

"Them Korean bitches will make me shower," Apache complained.

"Well, shit. See if Badger down for a quick handy, then."

One of Zombieland's more infamous residents, Horace, was sitting at the bar haggling with Puck, the recently promoted bartender, to add another beer to his tab. "We don't run tabs here, you jack ass. It's cash only," growled Puck. The bar likely served as a laundry for illicit cash, as well.

"I don't see those guys whipping out cash." Horace pointed at the Outlaws.

Puck yanked Horace's arm down and poured him a beer. "Drink this and be on your way while you still got legs to walk on."

Horace recognized leverage. "Add a Jack chaser…"

Puck had little to worry about. This arm of the club was all business. Even the muscle were subdued compared to the rest of the club. Puck, the ever-diplomatic bartender, relented and poured Horace the shot.

The ride captain for the Outlaws was Arthur B. Stranton III but everyone called him Bank, including the FBI. Bank's dad earned money the old-fashioned way; he inherited it. He sent his son to all the best boarding schools and Bank almost earned his masters from Wharton School of Business before his dad lost all his money the old-fashioned way: gambling, divorce lawyers, drinking, and whoring. He covered his losses for a few years, embezzling from the escrow accounts of his slip and fall clientele, stealing from Peter to pay Paul until there wasn't enough Peter to go around. A common problem/opportunity, according to one's proclivity, in Florida's aging communities. After a lengthy stay at Ocala Memorial, courtesy of a burly, disgruntled client, Arthur II was four-times divorced, disbarred, and interned in Federal Correctional Institution Coleman in Summerville.

Bitter, Arthur III turned to fighting, whores, drink, and petty cons to fund them, working his way down to the morose casinos of Alabama. Between brief stints at county lockups and a nickel, he reunited with his dad in Federal Prison in Summerville where his criminal financial education progressed exponentially. At the casino, he ran into the Outlaws. Arthur was foolish enough to beat Ax, the Outlaw's chapter president, at Texas Hold 'Em; and then, even more so, to actively gloat. His winnings were short lived, but he had found a home. Ax recognized talent, rage, and mettle. After kicking Bank's ass, Ax took Bank under his wing.

Bank secured an off-book Airbnb with a little extra cash incentive at 1111 Oak Forest Lane in Ormond Beach. The house was a tear down, but the owners kept it serviceable and rented it out to large, rowdy parties during spring break, NASCAR races, truck rallies, and Daytona's two large bike events. The Outlaws had a couple of permanent properties in the area, but Bank preferred to find a nonaffiliated location for his business. The Oak Forest property was a perfect safe house. It was just a mile or so away from the biker bars and campgrounds on Highway 1, and a block from the Loop, a favored biker scenic route. It sat directly on the intracoastal with a dock, slept 12 (according to Airbnb), and was in the middle of a crimefree, upscale, retiree neighborhood. The rest of the Outlaws would be staying in rented RV's and tents in one of the campgrounds on Highway 1. Bank also secured a modest-looking, overpowered, "fishing" boat with the rental. "Contingencies," Bank preached. What Bank did not know was that the Airbnb had been recently purchased by the NSA.

Horace slammed the shot and sipped his beer, treacherously eavesdropping on the Outlaws and catching bits and pieces of their conversation above the mid-day din of the bar. Too bright for his own good, he accurately surmised these were no ordinary bikers and rashly decided to check the bikers' saddlebags for treasure. He found them curiously unsecured and greedily placed the sum of their contents into two large, plastic, garbage bags he emptied from the nearby rodent infested dumpster.

CHAPTER EIGHT

Jack

Next door to the safe house sat a large home more typical of the area. It was built in the 1980's and remodeled in the 2000's. The owner had planted bamboo between his yard and his neighbors' yards. Over the years, it had grown some 15 feet tall and nearly as wide, invading much of one of the neighbors' poorly maintained yards. The owner was a wealthy, 60-year-old retiree named Jack. A private man, Jack lived alone. Few knew him or ever saw him out in public. Yet, given the paucity of available, ambulatory male targets in the area, a procession of over-perfumed widows and wealthy divorcees abandoned for trophy wives vied for his attention. They brought casseroles, pastas, pot roast, and fried chicken to his door on a near daily basis on the chance of Jack opening the door. Jack was cat nip for the old bitches and never lacked for a warm meal left at his door with an invitation for dinner and some cleverly coded derivative of clothing optional dessert. The neighbors speculated he was in the Mafia, CIA, witness protection, an assassin, GRU, Mossad, or notorious jewel thief. His mysterious past and reclusive nature made him an even more inviting target. Every single old biddy in a fifty-mile radius wanted to mount his privates above their headboard.

∞∞∞∞

Bank noticed three police cars closing in fast behind them as they were approaching the turn off Beach toward their safe house. Bank smartly rode on. The club followed. The police turned. Bank and the Outlaws circled back and stopped a block from the safe house. The cops had pulled into the neighbor's drive. Still wary, Bank instructed the club to ride the loop in order not to superfluously give away their safe house.

∞∞∞∞

Minutes before.
Michelle the housekeeper arrived at Jack's home. Jack called her "the maid" once. Michelle corrected him: "housekeeper". Jack was a Boomer and born before PC filters were standard equipment, back when the rule of the day was "sticks and stones..." and not "words are like grenades". A note was duct-taped to the door, sternly warning Michelle not to enter the garage and to call the police. She was puzzled, noting the sound of the Mercedes' engine purring within. "Masculine toxicity," Michelle mumbled. "Not even a 'please call the police, Michelle'."

∞∞∞∞

Florida's official motto is Sunshine State. A more apt motto might well be "God's waiting room". This was not the police's first rodeo. They called for the fire department and rescue. An officer took Michelle off to the side to question her. She knew little about Jack, other than he was a quiet man who paid well, in cash, and stayed out of her way while she cleaned. Nevertheless, enjoying the attention, she created a larger, fictional narrative. She did protest to the police officer that Jack called her "the maid". Feelings have taken on criminal weight. The officer took note. Michelle had a key to the home and provided it to the officer. The officer took her number and address and released her. Michelle stayed for the show but was escorted behind the crime tape with the other gathering onlookers, jockeying for the best position to video the event. Social media will be the decline of our civilization. No one can turn away from a train wreck and "likes" were digital currency, creating some of the most unlikely new celebrities and sucking the soul from the country.

Moments later, the Volusia County fire and rescue trucks arrived. The fireman stepped off the truck, geared up for the situation. Within seconds, Jack was removed from the car and laid on the far corner of the drive. No easy feat. Jack was a large man and, without a pulse, literally dead weight. The EMTs worked frantically and restored Jack's pulse and breathing before loading him into the ambulance alive, but still unresponsive. They raced away toward Advent Hospital. The gathered, mostly blue-haired, female crowd sobbed in disbelief and disappointment.

Jack wore darkness like a discount rack suit from Men's Warehouse. On the most cursory inspection, the fit and material were suitable. But, in the bright light of day, the cheap cut and flimsy fabric were visible to even the casual observer. Yet sadly, few even noticed or, worse yet, deigned to care. Our world is full of the self-obsessed, moral elitists consumed in a whirlwind of micro-aggressions and dynamic PC nonsense. Erstwhile, the real transgressions muddle on, unchecked by the ironically woke masses. Quoth the raven, nevermore and then proceed to croak unceremoniously in a puddle of body fluids in a ditch. Nobody cares, just use the correct fucking pronoun in the obit.

The Outlaws completed the 25-mile scenic loop of Old Florida. Ancient live oaks filter the sunlight through their massive branches draped with Spanish moss, forming a low arch above the narrow, winding road. The route is lined with native palms, perilously fronting the Halifax River, eroding its thin margins, and crosses one of the few remaining draw bridges over the Intracoastal. The fire truck and EMTs were gone, but the cops were still at the location. The Outlaws rode on, stopping at the Iron Horse on Highway 1. The bar was hopping, and the parking lot was jammed with custom bikes, sling shots, and classic bikes. As each year passed, more and more three-wheelers joined the ranks. Bikers are, sadly, a dying breed. Up front, a small section of the lot was roped off for the one-percenters. The "valet" waved the Outlaws into the reserved lot. Bank instructed One Eye to stay with the bikes. One Eye was both loyal and intimidating. In spite of their illicit payload, no further security was required and would only draw attention. One Eye found a table nearby in the shade and ordered a beer from a half-naked, left-behinder waitress.

Left-behinders were Daytona Beach spring breakers from back in its MTV heyday who had chosen to make spring break permanent by not returning home after their vacation, assuming the frivolity and debauchery would continue unencumbered by neither time nor money. There were five stages. Stage one was good times. Hanging at the beach by day and beach bars by night, crashing with spring break new arrivals, sampling tight, new flesh almost weekly. This was short lived. Stage two left-behinders found jobs at beach bars and restaurants. They pecked out a reasonable, if not enchanting, existence, as few new arrivals wanted to screw the broke-ass, sweaty help. Sadly, said jobs were boring and difficult and, consequently, filled with drug users which quickly led to bad decisions and a hellish descent to stage three. For women, some chose gentlemen's clubs or took housekeeping jobs at local hotels. Men were less fortunate and had to turn to manual labor jobs in construction or landscaping where they competed with illegals and received low wages and less than ideal work conditions. Florida summers are brutal. Drug usage increased with the frustration of the dream of an endless summer now completely eviscerated. The lucky ones returned home at this point to a forgiving family and, hopefully, a fresh start. Although, truth be told, the rate of recidivism was quite high. The stubborn, or those with no home to return to, descended into stage four. Stage four typically involved prostitution or drug dealing for the lucky ones and petty crimes for the less fortunate. Stage five was living on the street. Good news is that during Bike Week, even stage fivers in possession of the majority of their teeth and access to a shower could get a job peddling beer, drugs, or, at the very least, mucking human shit stalls.

One Eye's waitress was a stage three. She got thrust off the stage at the Diamond Club during Bike Week by the traveling A-team of strippers with their flawless skin, big eyes, perfectly engineered bodies, and deeply damaged souls until they left town for the next circus to splay their short-lived wares to pay the devil his share. The waitress had One Eye's attention. She brought him a cold, Bud heavy and offered an extended view of her ample, if not aged, wares, judged more harshly in the bright of day. One Eye bit his lip and reminded himself his duty. He dismissed the waitress unmolested in all but his mind.

The Iron Horse had a strict no colors rule which the Outlaws and the other "one-percenter" gangs routinely ignored. They stepped up to the crowded bar which, hastily and without verbalized grievance, made way for the bikers. These were of the 99-percenters, the weekend warriors: lawyers, doctors, CPAs, dentists, and other executives. They were wealthy enough to purchase $30,000 plus bikes, pay someone to trailer the bikes down while they themselves flew first class to Daytona for the week to act bad-ass and otherwise let their metaphorical hair down. They were a proud but aging breed looking for adventure, a t-shirt, and bragging rights... not conflict. Once upon a time, it was a reliable motto that what happened at Bike Week stayed at Bike Week. Well, everything but herpes. Technology ruined that illusion. Neglecting to disable photo sharing settings and the advent of social media and there were no more secrets and a lot of wealthy divorce lawyers, doctors, and accountants living in condos writing substantial alimony checks or searching the dark web for alternate but less expensive, albeit darker, solutions.

After a bit, Bank dispatched Apache out to spell One Eye and Badger to recon the safe house. A couple in a smart car with a license plate from Connecticut brazenly pulled into the "bike only" parking area. Both were of slight build and decked out in stereotypical tourist garb. The woman fearlessly approached Badger.

"Where did you get that cool retro jacket?" she asked. Badger scoffed.

"An Indian." The man pointed at the bike's distinctive logo. "Shouldn't that be Native American, honey?" he asked his partner.

"We're in Florida, dear," the woman replied. "Frigging barbarians down here. They voted for Trump and even have a white, republican governor for Christ's sake."

The man sighed. "I so would love Florida if not for the Floridians." They both giggled uncontrollably. The woman dropped her Louis Viton onto the gravel and bent from the waist to retrieve it, offering Apache an unobstructed view of her not unpleasant ass.

Apache growled. The couple were unmoved and continued to admire the bikes from a close distance until Apache shooed them away, but not before they placed a tiny, tracking device on the Indian. The couple entered the bar and wedged in between the Outlaws. Both were seasoned FBI agents. Sometimes the best disguise was to stand out from the crowd. The man ordered a round of craft beers for the Outlaws at the bar. The bartender served a round of Bud heavy. The woman ordered a frozen margarita. The bartender poured her a shot of tequila and unceremoniously dropped a cube of ice into the plastic cup. Bank recognized the agent's ploy and left the bar. The club members followed. Apache produced a knife and flattened two of the tires on the smart car. The agents remained in the bar, finishing their drinks to the bewildered stares of the remaining bikers. They were made and knew it.

The bartender presented the check for just under $500. The female agent handed him an American Express. The bartender scoffed and pointed over his shoulder at sign that read, "Cash only. All others will pay in ass or blood". The two agents looked at each other. The bartender produced a bat. "Florida," the female agent said. "How about $100 and a nice purse?"

The bartender looked at the male agent and said, "and the Rolex".

"That is a $15,000 watch," the agent responded.

"Give me a break. That's a knock-off, maybe worth a grand. Cops can't afford a Rolex. Just call it depreciation and I'll give another free round on the house."

"And I keep my purse," the female agent pleaded.

"Deal. But lady, it's a knock-off, as well."

The male agent scoffed. The female agent blushed as she recalled purchasing the item in the parking lot in Pisa, Italy from a North African street vendor. She shook hands with the bartender as the male agent reluctantly removed his watch to pay the tab. "Give it up for these two pigs. Another round on the house," yelled the bartender. The bar crowd roared. The bartender turned to the barback. "Dumbass doesn't know his watch is a real Rolex."

∞∞∞∞

Jack was awakened in the emergency room by an abrupt, intense pain in his crotch as the nurse carelessly yanked the catheter from his penis. Viewing wrinkly old man nut sacks was not her favorite part of the job but, unfortunately, a frequent one. It was Volusia County, after all, where the median age was 102-years-old. Jack's next memory was wrenching off the uncomfortable mask on his face and having it forcefully replaced. Jack would spend the next two days in ICU floating in and out of consciousness. On day three, he was discharged to a regular hospital bed with a full-time babysitter to monitor his every move and keep him away from visitors, electronic devices, and edible food.

"Ma'am." Jack tried to get the attention of the babysitter.

She looked up from her phone.

"I need to poop, lady."

The babysitter brought Jack a bed pan. "Neither one of us want to deal with the mess I'll make trying to use that." Jack tossed the bedpan to the floor. The clattering of the bedpan rapidly brought three reinforcements to the room. "You guys do know I'm not on the FBI's Most Wanted list?"

The charge nurse spoke in a rigid voice. "You tried to commit self-harm. We have certain protocols, including restraints, if necessary, Mr. Smith."

"Wait, what?" Jack responded; his mind still not clear.

"You have to empty your bowels into the pan." The charge nurse handed Jack the pan.

"Empty my bowels? You mean take a shit?" Jack smiled, skipped the middleman and promptly shit the bed. Jack had an issue with authority. "Now it's a party."

∞∞∞∞

Badger arrived at the safe house and texted Bank. "All good." Bank and the rest of the gang arrived at the house and began unloading their personal belongings and the merchandise.

"What the fuck?" Badger rejoined to the empty saddle bag.

Bank quickly checked the remaining bags. All empty. One Eye and Apache exchanged nervous glances.

One Eye spoke first. "I swear, Bank, I never took my eye off the bikes. Nobody came near them."

Apache, unfortunately, had a less definitive story. "Look, Bank. A couple of tourist types came over and were admiring the bikes, but I ran them off. But no way they stole the merch."

Bank nodded. Neither were the brightest bulb in the chandelier, but they were loyal. The "tourist types" Apache was referring to were probably undercover cops of some ilk Bank surmised and were the "tourists" in the bar. Bank grabbed a burner phone and walked out on the dock to make an unpleasant, situation update call to Ax, the chapter president.

CHAPTER NINE

Cougars and the American Dream

A Louie Vuitton purse sat in the chair adjacent to Karen at the Asian owned and operated nail salon. The owner's grandparents came to the States via the Catholic Relief Services as tweens, shortly before the fall of Saigon. Her mother seized the opportunity, studied hard, and, along with another kid from the orphanage, got a job in a nail salon where they learned the business. Over the years, the two married, saved religiously, and eventually opened this modest salon on Route 27. By retirement, they owned a dozen other salons in the suburbs of Orlando. They turned the business over to Sue, their only child, a first generation American.

Sue graduated with a Master's in Business Administration Degree from the University of Florida.

Her husband and business partner held a two-year degree in cosmetology from the local vo-tech. They had, through business savvy and hard work, grown the business to over 25 locations in the greater Orlando area. Sue still worked at least three shifts a week on the floor in the original store in addition to her responsibilities managing the chain. Sue believed in staying in touch with her customers, employees, and her roots. Her husband managed their largest store just outside the Villages and also worked the floor most days. They defined the American dream.

A phone rang in the Louie as Sue was finishing up Karen's mani-pedi. "Excuse me. I have to take this," Karen said loudly to Sue. Karen pointed to the phone to assist in her translation. Karen had no idea Sue, her nail tech, was a multi-millionaire, and a native-born English speaker. Karen was a mid-40's woman who could pass for mid-30's, thanks to a lucrative divorce settlement, a gifted plastic surgeon, a zealous avoidance of sunlight, and a ruthless personal trainer. Karen defined the genesis of the fall of the American dream. Everything is an entitlement.

"They arrested him. Thank God. I was so worried..." She paused and added, "... for my safety", as instructed on the Cougars-R-Us forum. Karen was referring to Jason, her 21-year-old boy toy/shit mucker. Karen depicted the very concept of cougar. Her genuine concern was losing her boy toy. He had packed his duffle and informed her he was leaving the state after he got his check from the farm that afternoon. "Heading west," was all he said. Being kept as a boy toy had considerable perks but Karen's controlling nature and homework assignments had worn thin. Jason was ready to move back into a trailer, get drunk, and get laid by women younger than his mother who did not insist on an orgasm every time they had sex.

Karen was having none of that. She had spent months refining Jason's wardrobe, manners, sexual prowess, and vocabulary in order to meet the high standards of the country club set. It was one thing to be great in the sack and to look good on her arm, but he needed to be able to play the part at some cursory level in public, as well. She had given up on Jason's golf game after the pro refunded her money after offering his sexual services in lieu of said refund after only one horrifically failed lesson. Karen accepted the offer, contingent on a trial run which the pro failed due to his advanced age of 35 and unfortunate left hook.

Karen ran with a pride of cougars that shared advice on best practices to keep a young man satisfied and, failure to do that, ensnared in a relationship. The forum suggested, for a short-term desperation tactic, to have the target Marchman Acted and confined in a mental hospital to give him time to reconsider his decision. Desperate times and all. Further, his confinement would require the cougar's assistance to escape the immoral clutches of the for-profit mental health system. Cougars don't play. They are entitled a return on their investment. Given Karen's looks and willingness to go the extra mile, she found a deputy sheriff to act as her second in front of the judge, swearing he witnessed Jason abusing Karen under the influence of drugs and alcohol. The deputy sheriff was handsomely rewarded with Karen's not insignificant oral skills.

With a fresh French mani-pedi, Karen exited the salon after leaving Sue a generous tip of $1 in change. With a grateful heart, she paused at the door, almost forgetting her manners, and spoke loudly to Sue in pidgin: "Me thankie you."

Sue sighed and put the tip in the Catholic Relief Services jar she kept as a reminder to be grateful, even to assholes, of her parents' hard work and sacrifice. America, she thought, land of opportunity and entitled assholes with no appreciation for the great country they had inherited.

CHAPTER TEN
Gaia's Takedown

Back at Foul Balls, Emmitt and Jesus were wrestling with Gaia to get her cuffed without further offense of naked lady bits. A squadron of cell phones videoed their every move. Finally cuffed, each of the officers grabbed an elbow and carried her out, squirming like an angry toddler, to the morgue van. Jesus wrestled with trying to unlock the van and control the feral, naked lady; perhaps an oxymoron. The bar crowd spilled outside in spite of explicit instructions to the contrary. A mobile unit from WESH Channel 2 drove up and a camera person filled the morgue van with light, blinding the officers. Emmitt found an old, moldy body bag, cut the top and bottom out, and zipped Gaia up inside. Jesus rode in the back to keep the thrashing about to a minimum and was rewarded with a bite to the forearm. Jesus asked for a first aid kit as Gaia had drawn blood.

Emmitt laughed. "In a decommissioned morgue van? More likely to find Jimmy Hoffa."

"Who?"

The reporter, a young, attractive, Hispanic woman, smelled an Emmy. She jumped Emmitt as he tried to enter the van, blocking his path. The reporter showed Emmitt the video of his hands cupped around Gaia's breast. "What do you have to say about your abhorrent behavior, officer?"

Emmitt was pissed but remembered his two hours of media training and tried to smile while speaking in a clear, non-confrontational voice. "We don't comment regarding ongoing investigations." The smile came out creepy, like a clown from the movie "It". Emmitt was unaccustomed to media attention. The lights were blinding, and he didn't know where to look.

The interview video, cut together with the groping video, and video of shadowy figures tussling in the back of the morgue van, ending with Emmitt's creepy smile footage was picked up by CNN and MSNBC and replayed ad nauseum. This was coupled with the reporter's uninformed description of the incident focusing on yet another occasion of police brutality on a person of color. Gaia was Italian. Never let the facts get in the way of a good story and all. The reporter was offered, and subsequently accepted, a position at CNN the following day. CNN recognized a reporter with passion and a talent for unabashedly creating "facts" to fit the popular narrative.

Emmitt radioed dispatch for instructions with the glare of the camera's lights filling the van's cab. The sergeant on duty was familiar with Gaia and accurately ascertained the situation. He instructed Emmitt to transport her to the Pines for a mandatory 72-hour observation. The duty sergeant wanted no part of this circus at the station on his watch.

Emmitt raced away from Foul Balls with the morgue van's lights flashing, hoping to get a head start on the news van. He took the first right turn while simultaneously killing the lights, and then the next left, throwing the news van off his scent. Unfortunately, the news producer back at the station was monitoring the police scanner and had relayed their destination to the reporter. The WESH news van, along with three other stations, were set up and waiting for the morgue van's arrival. Two news helicopters hovered overhead dangerously low, creating a whirlwind of debris and noise. The other stations used WESH's erroneous report as a confirmed source and crosschecked the solitary source using each other as secondary and tertiary confirmed sources. A not uncommon practice among media types looking for a sensational story that fits the agreed upon narrative du jour. But facts, right? Long since a casualty to ratings in the news game.

Gaia caught Jesus square in the face with a kick, bloodying his nose. Emmitt opened the van's door, flood lit from a half dozen cameras and the two encircling helicopters. Gaia continued to violently struggle as they extricated her from the morgue van. Wind from the helicopters blew off her modified body bag. All the stations reported Jesus's bloodied face and forearm, as well as Gaia's nudity as further evidence of police brutality and sexual misconduct. Her feral screams of, "All you bastards can suck my tiny dick," were drowned out by the helicopters as Emmitt and Jesus struggled to get Gaia inside the relative sanity of the mental hospital.

The WESH reporter proudly displayed her Emmy in her new cubicle at CNN. She had scored an unobstructed view of the Olympic Ring Fountain. Journalistic integrity. The greatest oxymoron for this generation.

CHAPTER ELEVEN

The Outlaws Purdue and Swede

Bank pulled Purdue aside at the Outlaw safehouse to game the possible whereabouts of the missing heroin. The rest of the crew was busy sorting an ever-growing pile of supplies delivered by Amazon and the local Budweiser beer distributor. Purdue was the chapter's "product manager".

Purdue began his criminal career as a big pharma rep for Purdue Pharmaceuticals, the largest distributor of Oxy. He finagled the job networking with his father's golfing buddies at the ultra-exclusive Atlanta Athletic Country Club founded in 1898. Purdue graduated in the bottom quartile of his class at the University of Georgia, but with his top one percent connections, was admitted to the UGA's School of Medicine in Augusta,

Georgia. He was a scratch golfer, gifted philanderer, and a world class drinker, but had never opened a textbook. He washed out the first semester. Hard work was not in his DNA and even his dad's connections only reached so far. Purdue quickly realized his job as a Purdue pharma rep was pushing legalized heroin, and there was definitely an exploding street market for oxy. With his father's connections, Purdue had access to any private golf course in the Southeastern United States. Purdue invited doctors to play at the exclusive courses. He bet the shady ones oxy scripts. He bet the ethical ones large dollars which he then converted to oxy scripts on the 19th hole at settlement time. Soon he was making double his salary selling oxy at bars, country clubs, casinos, and restaurants across the southeast. As with most, it is greed that was Purdue's demise, and he got pinched selling to an undercover agent in a casino in Montgomery, Alabama. It was there he met Ax in the town lockup. Purdue was only there overnight before his dad sprung him, but Ax smelled talent, rage, and mettle. Purdue was short on mettle and rage, but long on talent. The two talked all night.

The bike club's primary source of revenue was meth, but sales were slipping. Seemed everyone and their inbred cousins could and did cook meth, creating an oversupply and driving prices down. Ax asked about selling oxy. Purdue explained that soon the government would crack down on oxy scripts and the supply would dwindle, skyrocketing the cost. Not a long-term business model. Ax was about to lose interest until Purdue added: "But heroin, though." All those oxy addicts would be turning to heroin to satisfy their opioid addiction at a fraction of the cost. That's the future. Heroin. Purdue explained the profit margins on heroin were much higher than oxy and the product virtually unfettered by government control. All you need is a connection.

Ax wasn't sure about Purdue's club worthiness but took his information. It's not like a club member could ride bitch or in a side car. Bad optics. Eventually, Ax hooked Purdue up in a subordinate motorcycle club and, after a couple years, Purdue earned his Outlaw patch and became a trusted member of the club at the highest levels for his business savvy, marketing skills, and product knowledge.

∞∞∞∞

"So, where you see our weak spots?" Bank asked.

Purdue had already thought this out. "Only place we left the product unattended is the last place we touched it...Foul Balls. Gotta be where it was pinched."

"Damn it! That's on me. What you think, a rival gang or just a crime of convenience?"

"Hard to be sure, but I'm betting the latter," Purdue responded.

"Okay. So how do we find and, more importantly, retrieve the heroin?"

"That shit was pure. Let's get Swede to hack into the hospital admissions in Ocala for that day and pull on that string first."

"Or the morgue," Bank replied. They both laughed. "Yup, that string is going to be more difficult to pull." Bank's thoughts turned dark. "God forgives..."

Purdue finished. "...Outlaws don't."

Swede was an Army Vet trained and highly skilled in cyber security. Now he was the chapter's resident hacker and delivered in no time. Hospital cyber security is virtually non-existent. Any eleven-year-old could hack into his mom's plastic surgery records for blackmail material while simultaneously playing video games and whacking off in the basement to Anime lesbian porn. Swede had a list of eighteen names that had been transported to Ocala Memorial in the last three days for heroin overdoses. Ten left horizontally via the loading dock, unclaimed by family members to be entombed in Marion County's rapidly expanding Paupers' cemetery. One county commissioner had brazenly motioned for a corner of the landfill to be reserved for expanding the Paupers' cemetery. "Perhaps the top layer." It did not receive a second, only for lack of courage. There was little sympathy in the county for the drug crowd. Five victims were in a coma and two were in ICU. Swede found an 18th victim who was transported from the ER to The Pines, the local loony bin. It was China's 31st visit.

After receiving Swede's news, Purdue and Bank immediately traveled back to Ocala. They brought One Eye along in case of trouble. Purdue had his colors, but still was not much help in a scuffle and was useless in a gun fight. His value for this mission was, with a quick shave and haircut, he could pass as a normal citizen, and he knew his way around the medical system. First stop was Foul Balls to replace the motorcycles with the less conspicuous truck.

Normally just over a 90-minute ride, Bike Week was heating up and Highway 40 to Ocala was a popular ride. Some three hours later, they pulled into Foul Balls for a friendly chat with Earl. He could not be ruled out as being a conspirator in the theft. Earl, until recently a fixture at the bar, was nowhere to be found. Puck slid three beers to the bikers. "Yeah, Earl got canned for using money out of the till to talk Gaia out of beating some poor, accidental tourist to death. He's shoveling shit over at the farm," Puck explained, with a bit too much glee. Puck bar-backed for Earl, and Earl was stingy on sharing the tips but generous with jabs regarding Puck's acne-inspired nickname.

"That tracks." The club was very familiar with Gaia. "Which farm?" Bank asked.

"Beats me. I just know the bastard is shoveling shit."

One Eye backhanded Puck to refresh his memory. Puck wiped the blood from his nose.

Bank asked Puck again with similar results achieved but stopped One Eye from inflicting further violence. "The dumbass don't know," Bank said to One Eye. "Puck, how 'bout you help One Eye with a list of possible farms and addresses."

"I can just call him," Puck suggested, nervously polishing the bar top with the bloodied rag, giving the bar top a sheen of hepatitis C, a taste of HIV, and a haze of antibiotic-resistant bacterial staph infection.

"This is more of an unannounced face-to-face conversation. One Eye, take Puck's phone before you leave."

CHAPTER TWELVE
Jack Enters the Bin

Early on day two of Jack's hospital stay, he spoke, in a moment of semi-lucidity, with a physiatrist via an iPad for two minutes. The shrink made an informed, professional opinion based on the lengthy and thorough two-minute examination that Jack was at further risk of harming himself and/or others. More importantly, the tele-shrink enlarged his bank account by $250. The shrink subsequently Baker Acted Jack. The Act, as intended, has value. Two family members can go in front of a judge and, after presenting evidence, request a "loved one" be forcibly held for 72-hours for observation. The Act also lays out responsibilities of the mental health facility and patient/inmate rights. But, like most laws, the Act was manipulated for other purposes, mainly profit. A similar act, The Marchman Act, dealt more with drug addicts and fear of harm to others and was likewise misused, mostly for profit, revenge, and spite.

On day four, Jack was pronounced medically fit and was discharged from the hospital. He arrived at The Pines midafternoon via a secured, non-emergency medical transport vehicle staffed by two burly goons. "Who the hell did I murder?" Jack thought to himself. He was dressed in an ill-fitting hospital gown sans knickers. The goons supplied a blanket more to safeguard their seat from shit stains from the old geezer than the protection of Jack's dignity.

They escorted Jack in, one on either side, discreetly pinning his arms should the 60-year-old, barefoot, half-naked Jack make a mad dash for freedom. Blessedly, for all involved, the goons draped the blanket around his shoulders, covering his bare ass. There were two sets of doors. One locked behind the other. Images of One Flew Over the Cuckoo's Nest came over Jack. This was a loony bin. "Where is Chief?" Jack asked the receptionist. The receptionist did not smile.

"Generational thing, I guess," Jack shrugged. The receptionist scoffed. "Soylent Green factory?" Jack asked. The receptionist scowled. Patients to the Bin were less than human to the staff. They were product, and unseemly ones at that. Much like a hog at a slaughterhouse with only a slightly better outcome for the product but much higher margins for the house.

Jack was old enough to remember when shrinks employed shock therapy, lobotomies, and tooth extraction to cure an assortment of mental illnesses to include homosexuality, postpartum depression, and bipolar disorder. Modern mental health professionals now favor psychoactive drugs that turn patients into easily manipulated zombies but won't rule out the occasional shock therapy for old times' sake. Fortunately, the settled science of tooth extraction as a treatment had been abandoned. Even now, with little due process, for-profit mental institutions can hold patients against their will almost indefinitely. Jack consequently held a deep-seated mistrust of the mental health system. The better one's insurance plan was, the more danger one faced. Jack's health plan was gold-plated.

The receptionist called for admissions while the goons impatiently waited at Jack's side. Jack had a congenital heart condition along with hypertension. Given the situation, both his pulse and blood pressure were out of control, making him jittery. Patients quickly learned nothing happens fast at The Pines. Some 15 minutes later, a man wearing scrubs came through a third locked door to escort Jack to Admissions. There, the masked Jack was directed to urinate in a cup. Jack removed his blanket and placed it onto the wet countertop, promptly soaking the blanket. After finishing the task at hand, Jack wrapped the soaking wet blanket around him and handed the pee cup to the attendant. Jack found a seat in a small, dark, empty lobby outside admissions and was instructed to wait. "Embrace the suck," Jack whispered to himself.

Shortly thereafter, a young man in street clothes was escorted in by a police officer talking jibber jabber loudly to himself or an imaginary friend. Perhaps both. He was expedited to the ward. Jack's blood pressure climbed. An hour passed. A young lady who Jack was later to learn was Dakota, arrived sobbing and escorted by two EMTs from a neighboring county. She, too, was wearing only a hospital gown sans underwear. The admissions office expedited her admission. A second hour passed while Jack shivered in the wet blanket, heart racing.

"How much longer?" Jack asked the employee. "I'm not feeling well," he added. His whole body was jittering from the cold and his racing heart.

"Another hour or so," was the reply from the compassionate employee. They had heard it all and the jitters was just a sign of alcohol or drug addiction withdrawals. Jack had neither.

Jack protested mildly, seeing no win in pissing off those with the power to retain you indefinitely. Shortly after, two more patients arrived. An admissions person placed one in a private, unmonitored room; a serious Backer Act protocol violation Jack was later to learn. One of dozens. Finally, a large, unsympathetic woman came out and handed Jack a fistful of papers to fill out and sign. Jack protested his inability to read without his glasses.

"Look, cotton top. You been out here bitching, now get these damn papers filled out and signed so we can get you processed in." She spoke angrily, seemingly offended by Jack's presence. Or maybe she was just out of bacon.

Jack could squint and make out the headlines, but the regular print was just a blur. He filled the papers out the best he could but, without his wallet, cell phone, or glasses, left many sections blank and signed them all as "Shrimp Johnson". Years ago, he signed these kinds of forms as George Washington Carver, a brilliant, Black scientist who single-handedly saved the economy of the agrarian South by finding numerous uses for peanuts. Jack stopped using Carver's name because he was told that it was racist. The definition of racism grows at a pace faster than Moore's Law. He did recognize one form stating he was voluntary committing himself. He signed that one in block letters using his non-dominant hand: "HILLARY CLINTON."

An attendant escorted him down a long hallway to ward three. Ward two was for veterans with PTSD, some of which never having been deployed. Perhaps suffering from misuse of personal pronouns. Ward four was for the more dangerous of the crazies. Jack's ward, three, was the less violent, run of the mill nut jobs. Ward one was a ghost ward; never spoken of, and the inmates inhabiting it never seen. It was speculated they had excellent health plans with no known relatives. The inmates of the other wards and employees alike referred to the ghost ward residents as "cash cows". All the wards were unisex and had double rooms with bathrooms closed off by a half door.

The duty nurse for the ward asked a young, female colleague to join her to strip search Jack. It was her third day on the job. The young nurse visibly recoiled. "Please don't ruin that poor child's sex life," Jack begged. The nurse selected another victim, likewise disgusted, but much older, less innocent to the process and further evolved in her sex life.

Jack sat on a cold, stainless-steel table while the nurse took his vitals. She mumbled, "normal temperature, 135...pulse kind of high, blood pressure 200 over 110, oh shit. You have high blood pressure?"

"You think?" Jack responded.

The nurse smirked. "Don't sass me, old man. Did you take your meds today?"

"No," Jack curtly replied.

She shrugged, motioning Jack to get off the table and drop his blanket and gown. She grabbed the wet "clothing" for disposal and shrieked. "This better not be urine!"

Jack was tempted to say it was but replied truthfully. "Nope. Just water. No one else seemed to mind I was soaked." She gave a cursory examination of his trembling body but, fortunately for the both of them, did not perform any cavity searches. Jack hadn't shit since the bed incident. A finger up his ass might have yielded more delights than she bargained for. She gave Jack two ill-fitting gowns without closure strings, AKA weapons, and released him into the wild of the psych ward without further ado.

"Embrace the suck," Jack whispered over and over and over. The ward was chaos. He took an empty seat in the day room, trying not to offer a glimpse of his hairy balls to the coed crowd speaking loudly, competing for attention over the television set, the staff, and the other inmates.

Six hours later, a second nurse took Jack's vitals. "Holy shit," she whispered excitedly and raced off. Jack clamped his legs shut. She returned shortly with an emergency blood pressure medication and a small paper cup of water. "Take this and, for God's sake, keep your legs together."

"My nuts doth offend?" Jack asked.

CHAPTER THIRTEEN
Barnes and Noble

At FBI headquarters in Orlando, the sham tourists explained they had likely been made by the Outlaws.

"Damn it, Barnes. Rookie mistake or did you flash your badge to pick up a chick," inquired the SAC (Special Agent in Charge).

"I would never…" Barnes began to reply but paused as Noble rolled her eyes. "If it was just for one chick," Barnes weakly protested. The SAC shook his head, wondering again why the hell these two clowns were assigned this case.

"It was at the Iron Horse," Barnes added, as though the location explained away his behavior. He and Noble smiled inaptly at their failed mission. "Bank." That explained everything to the SAC.

"What's with the smirking, jackasses? You think you should still get a participation trophy?" the SAC inquired.

A subordinate technical agent had entered the room. Neither Barnes nor Noble were familiar with the agent, but both noticed he carried himself with more self-assurance than a typical desk jockey. "Your agents managed to plant a tracker on one of the Outlaws' bikes. We got the safe house," explained the tech agent.

The SAC instructed Barnes and Noble to find a suitable location near the safe house for surveillance.

"On it, sir," Noble replied. The SAC had given them their code names. They were his least favorite agents because of their unconventional tactics, tendency to take shortcuts, and thick public complaint files. Yet so, they were his most successful agents and their assignment to this case had come from higher authorities.

"And change your damn clothes," the SAC shouted as they left. "Before I put you in a minivan with a broken AC and assign you to undercover meter maid duty at Disney World looking for knock off OLD Navy smugglers." Orlando was not the SAC's dream assignment. He hated tourists and traffic; a daily, year-round double feature in Orlando. But he was the SAC during the Pulse Night Club shooting and lost any chance of promotion. He would die, retire, or get fired in Orlando without a major, earth shattering, international front-page kind of bust. It was a difficult fate to swallow, and the SAC grew more cantankerous and demanding by the day. "In Florida and not a beach in sight." It is like a hungry man watching a fat man eat a steak through a window.

The tech, on temporary duty from the NSA to the FBI, motioned for Barnes and Noble to follow. He made no mention of this to the agents as he closed the door to his office, flipped his monitor around and handed Barnes a file. "This," he pointed to a house on the monitor, "… is the Outlaws' safe house. Next door," he pointed to Jack's house, "…is the perfect location for surveillance. The jacket has the details of both homes including the name and contact information of the surveillance house owner. Some old dude who lives alone."

"Thanks, dude. That'll save us some time."

"Hold your thanks. The owner is in the Bin in Ocala." Barnes nor Noble thought to acknowledge the tech's unprecedented efficiency, nor the fact the lowly tech had an office with a window.

"The Bin?" Noble asked.

The tech smirked. "The pejorative for The Pines, as in Loony Bin, the private mental hospital. They're well known…for their high profit margins. Not for their standard of care, to be clear."

"Perfect," Noble replied. "They hold everyone at least five days for the insurance money. With a phone call, we can easily get them to extend Jack's stay through Bike Week. We can just borrow his house."

"B and E?" Barnes asked. Noble nodded yes. "I love it when a plan comes together," Barnes replied.

The tech held up his hand. "Slow your roll. The Old Dude's jacket, other than contact information, is completely redacted." Neither Barnes nor Noble ever thought to ask the tech why he already knew so much about the homeowner.

CHAPTER FOURTEEN

The Outlaw One Eye Appoints a New Foul Balls Bartender

One Eye and Puck found Earl on their second try mucking stalls at Jason's old farm. Earl was eager to cooperate, a little too eager for One Eye's liking. "It was Puck," Earl announced shakily, without prompt.

"What was Puck?" One Eye inquired. "I ain't asked you nothing."

"I told you he was shady as hell," offered Puck.

One Eye slammed Puck to the floor of the stall and held his boot on Puck's neck while he was face down in a giant horse turd. "And I told you to keep your trap shut." He released his boot long enough for Puck to draw a breath of foul air before forcibly placing it back down. "I asked, what was Puck?"

Earl looked at Puck squirming in the muck, conjuring a suitable confession that would not get him beaten or murdered. A little manure in his face would be unpleasant, but he could deal with that. "I saw Puck talking furtively to a tourist couple a few nights back. I don't know what they were talking about, but one of the tourists handed him a card and some cash."

"Furtively? Where did you find that word...the FBI, DEA, ATF? And what makes you think that is why I'm here? Maybe I just missed you serving me watered-down drinks at Foul Balls and wanted to drop by for a social call or a friendly hello." One Eye had released his hold on Puck and was strolling around the barn collecting a couple ropes. Earl pissed his pants.

Puck, with a face full of horseshit, looked up at Earl. "You pissed your pants, man," Puck exclaimed while maniacally laughing.

Earl looked down at his pants in shame. "Well you shit your face, Puck," retorted Earl.

One Eye casually formed a noose in both ropes as he continued to speak. "Earl, might you have spoken with someone regarding our plans to park the trailers at Foul Balls?"

Earl paused. One Eye looped the noose around his neck. "Hell no. I mean, I mightta coulda let something slip to some broad, but what does it matter?" One Eye headbutted Earl and knocked him to the stall's floor. Earl looked up. "Puck was working that day. Boss man fired me for losing $100 bill out of the till."

One Eye suddenly recalled a stranger pointing at them while they were talking to Puck at the bar. "Who was that dude pointing at us, Puck?"

"What the hell you talkin' about, One Eye?"

Puck's face was replanted in the horseshit. One Eye removed his boot from Puck's neck and kicked him in the ribs. "The asshole pointing at us the day we dropped the trailers off at the bar."

"You mean Horace? He's just a harmless junkie."

"Where can I find this harmless junkie called Horace that you speak of?" One Eye knew junkies and their propensity to take mad risk for a fix. "Can you take me to him?" One Eye casually flipped the second noose around Earl's neck and drew it tight.

"Horace'll be where the drugs be. He floats around all those trash trailer parks looking for handouts."

"You mean Zombieland?"

Puck and Earl silently confirmed, both nodding in agreement.

"Guess we are done here, mates."

One Eye sighed and walked out of the stall with the end of the ropes in hand. A smart man might think to remove the ropes from about one's neck. Earl and Puck weren't that bright and, for the moment, were still shaking from terror. The rev of the motorcycle got their attention as their manure-covered eyes locked in silent, belated recognition. "Oh, shit," they screamed as they were dragged out of the stall, bouncing against the walls and various bladed farm implements.

CHAPTER FIFTEEN
Double Cross

Fate favors the foolish. Hell, even Jesus saved two career criminals on their death crosses just for uttering, "my bad, I get it now. You the man." Erstwhile, some dude across town who fed the poor and tended the sick his entire life is neck deep in feces for eternity 'cause he never uttered the magic words.

A farm implement, called a harrow, sliced into both Earl and Puck's shit-covered bodies, and mercifully cut the tow rope as well before the two were strangled. Neither were critically injured but both had lost their britches, boots, and a significant amount of blood. Their wounds were literally smeared with horse piss and manure. One Eye continued on, disconnecting the tow rope at the end of the twisting, tree-canopied, dirt road without thought as to the fate of Earl and Puck.

Smart men, or even reasonable ones, would be thankful to be alive and seek medical attention. Earl and Puck chose a different path. Earl crawled over to Puck and began choking him. "You ugly ass bastard. You almost got us killed." Sunlight filtered in from the tin roof, highlighting the dust surrounding the noosed men in the otherwise darkened barn. It was like a scene from a well-produced spaghetti western.

Puck located a wrench and swung it wildly at Earl, connecting with his forearm with enough force to dislocate his grip. Earl fell over, gripping Puck's arm. Puck full-mounted Earl, pinning his arms with Puck's knees. Puck raised the heavy wrench in preparation to deliver what would likely be a deadly blow but was brusquely interrupted by a bullet whizzing by his ear followed shortly by the loud retort of the farmer's pistol.

"Damn, I missed. What you two shit stains doing in my barn, anyway?" The farmer didn't recognize the shit-covered Earl and was unfamiliar with Puck.

"I'm Earl, sir."

"The new shit mucker?"

Earl nodded in reply.

"That tracks. And the naked fellow about to kill you or hate fuck you? Don't reckon I know which would be worse."

"That's my friend Puck," Earl replied. Puck dropped the wrench on Earl's head. "Damn, dude."

"Hmph." The farmer smiled. "Might want to get some new friends. Why you suppose he want to kill you?"

"I reckon 'cause I tried to kill him first."

"Hmph. Reason enough, I suppose." The farmer nodded his head. "Maybe I can do the two of you a solid and shoot you both. I got a gun, a hundred acres, a bag of lime and a shovel." He waved the pistol at them.

Earl protested needlessly. "Wait. I may have a proposal for you." The farmer was bluffing. He would not have gone to the trouble of killing the likes of these two.

Earl whispered something in Puck's ear. He heard rumors around the barn the farmer was having some financial difficulties after losing a large "fixed" wager and was juggling debtors to keep both them and the bookie's henchmen at bay. Earl sat up. "We have a financial deal we would like for you to consider."

"You two losers don't have the money to buy a crack whore a cigarette to give you a handy."

Puck looked puzzled. "Why I pay for a handy, anyway?" He raised both of his shit-covered hands. "Not like these don't function for free."

Earl punched Puck in the shoulder. "While true, we do have some information of value."

The farmer was running low on options. What could it hurt to hear them out, he thought to himself. "Alright, what bullshit scheme you two losers come up with?" the farmer asked aloud.

"It's a little shady."

"Color me surprised."

"We know where a half million of unguarded heroin is being stored."

"Then why tell me? Get it for yourself and sell it."

"Cause the owners of said product would immediately suspect us. Never you. And to be honest, we would likely kill ourselves using it before we sold it. We will go get the heroin and sell it to you for a quarter million dollars and get the hell out of Dodge before the owners' know what's what."

"Who are these said owners?"

Earl and Puck exchanged nervous glances. "The Knights of Columbus," Puck answered without much thought.

The farmer laughed. "That right? I'm their president. Although we could use bigger Bingo prizes." He mused.

There was no good answer. Anyone with that much heroin was a badass and would take unkindly to it being stolen. Earl answered honestly. "The Outlaws."

"Fuck off. I'll just let you two bleed out or you can finish up your duel."

"$100,000, then."

"How about I give you ten dollars and an ambulance ride."

"Come on, man. We have to leave the country, or they will find us, torture us, and make us give you up. You got to make it worth our while."

The farmer thought for a minute. "You two dimwits even got passports?"

Puck and Earl looked at each other and collectively shook their heads no. The plan was in its infancy.

"Okay you two stupid shit stains. Here's the deal. I got a plane. I'll give you $10,000 and a plane ride to Nassau for the dope. Final offer, take it or get the hell out of my barn the best you can."

The two looked at each other, calculating they could live a couple years off that mountain of cash in the Bahamas, and collectedly nodded in agreement to the farmer's offer.

CHAPTER SIXTEEN
Dr. Bilbo aka Purdue

Purdue parked the truck in the doctor's lot at Orlando Memorial and exited the truck wearing a recently purchased stethoscope slung around the neck of his scrubs and a Wal-Mart name tag declaring him as a trainee named Bilbo. He wore a long-sleeved t-shirt underneath the scrubs to cover his tattoos. Purdue tailgated a nurse in through the employee entrance and had no trouble accessing the hospital's ICU ward. Last count, there were seven heroin OD cases in the hospital from the weekend, five of whom were in a coma and two who were conscious but in the ICU.

Purdue asked the nurse for help logging into the system. She complied without looking up. Doctors were notorious for forgetting their passwords. Unfortunately, two more of the OD cases had died and two others self-discharged without addresses on record. "Shit."

The nurse stole a glance at Purdue. "Bilbo?"

Purdue laughed. "Doctor Bilbo to you. Must have grabbed my stepson's ID. Who the hell names their kid Bilbo, right?" The nurse coquettishly giggled. Purdue cleaned up nicely. "Rough night with Ginger."

"Your wife?"

"Hell no, Crown and Ginger. Hey, any of those heroin overdoses from the weekend gonna make it out of their comas?"

"I don't know, Dr. Bilbo, are they?" She was getting skeptical regarding Dr. Bilbo's bona fides. She had never seen him in ICU, and she was pretty sure she would remember Dr. Bilbo.

"I only ask 'cause that one in 3A is kind of cute and I need a date that likes to party for my sister's wedding in Cabo this weekend." Purdue was always a good salesperson and could read a room.

"Aren't you married?" the nurse asked.

"Your point?" he retorted, as the nurse covertly covered her ring finger. Purdue was considered eye candy to those who liked the rugged, alpha male type.

The doors to ICU flung open. "Got another one from the Bin. Head injury. I think it looks worse than it is," yelled the EMT. Dakota's head was bandaged and seeping blood, but she was conscious. The nurse assigned her to a room and got her settled in and hooked up to a variety of mostly useless but billable pieces of equipment. Purdue followed the nurse in, hoping to pump her for more information if not just pump her. She was kind of hot and Purdue had a thing for nurses. Something about uncovering hidden treasures underneath the shapeless scrubs that rocked his boat. No reason to waste the visit entirely.

"Where are you, sweetie?" the nurse asked Dakota.

"The hospital."

"Today's date?"

"I really don't know."

"How did you get here?"

"Ambulance," Dakota shrugged.

"Where did you come from?"

"The Pines."

Purdue's ears perked up, connecting the dots. Pumping the nurse would have to wait. The nurse exited the room to go schedule an array of useless appointments with doctors and therapists who tipped generously for her "patient referrals" who they never had to actually see but could apply billable hours to insurance companies for. The insurance companies received federal grants in excess of the insurance company's fees for promoting the public's health when they approved such requests. Incidentally, those approving the federal grants were heavy investors in the insurance companies. The mob was small time compared to the health care racket. The nurse's exit left Purdue alone with Dakota. He turned on his charm. "Dakota. What a lovely name for a lovely young girl."

"Thank you?" Dakota was a bit taken aback. She was unaccustomed to men like Purdue flirting with her.

"The Pines, huh? I hear it is kind of a hellhole," Purdue deduced accurately based on the evidence lying in front of him.

"Yup."

"You meet a lady named China in there, per chance? Heroin overdose, I believe?"

Dakota propped herself up on her elbows struggling to focus her eyes and studied Purdue's face. "Isn't there some kind of law about doctors revealing medical information to third parties?" Dakota asked, recalling her lessons in the day room from Jack.

Purdue laughed and pointed at his Wal-Mart name tag. "Who the hell's a doctor?"

CHAPTER SEVENTEEN
Bin Therapy

After a belated lunch of unseasoned, rubberized chicken, cold rice with the consistency, appearance and flavor of maggots, and a cold slice of moldy bread, the staff called a mandatory group session to discuss the "minor incident" that had sent Dakota to the hospital, Jason to his own personal living hell, and of most concern to the inmates, delayed their gourmet meal. Housekeeping, such as it was, had made a cursory effort to clean the battlefield of the lion's share of solid waste and had successfully smeared the liquid remains into a haze of a curiously agreeable shade of salmon.

Stephanie's credentials were hazy. She never really claimed, with any level of certainty, to be anything more than a warm body in ill-fitting clothing. It was just inferred she was a therapist. Her name tag read, in bold letters "MANDATORY REPORTER", but her actual name changed on an as needed basis. She was a mid-fifties woman of significant girth, failing to yield to her current reality. Self-delusion is an admirable quality in a therapist. For the occasion, Steph selected baby blue stilettos, an engineering coup into itself, with a short, matching skirt, a sheer white blouse that revealed an ill-fitting corresponding bra creating a disquieting illusion of two heavily-veined, overripened, albino cantaloupes on the cusp of eruption.

After passing out paper and a pencil of non-lethal dimensions to each of the inmates, Steph took a seat, displaying her equally challenged spanks to those who were unfortunate enough to have selected a seat in an opposing direction exceeding ninety degrees. Stephanie began. "Do we think our behavior today was appropriate?"

Wheels quickly responded. "If 'we' is you, as always the answer is 'no'. But I think I can speak for the group that we are thankful you are at least wearing underwear today."

Steph sighed and crossed her legs, exposing more thigh but less crotch, yet expanding the toxic splash zone by twenty percent. "The royal 'we', Derrick."

"So both you and us?"

"No, just you guys," Steph said, frustrated.

"Whoa, Steph. That's a lot to unpack. First off, its 2021. You can't say 'guys'. There are like 72 genders. Get woke. Secondly, if you just meant us inmates, don't be dishonest. Just say what the hell you mean. But, to get to your point, generally speaking, as I can't speak for these losers, my behavior was on point. Yours and the staff at this hellhole, not so much."

"What makes you think your fellow patients are losers, Derrick?" Steph asked, ignoring the meatier parts of Wheels' statement.

Wheels maniacally laughed. "Look at 'em. And I am not snubbing you from the loser category."

"That's not a very nice thing to say, Derrick."

"Nice. Aren't you supposed to be a psychiatrist? Seek and speak the truth and all that bullshit, Stephanie. Anyone in this literal shit-stained room look like a winner to you? Grab a mirror, I'll include you in my hypothesis. And I have spent more time with these losers than all you overeducated, haughty, ignorant shrinks put together. You guys spend your day in the break room drinking coffee, swapping cruel stories about the crazies on the ward, listening to Nickelback, and watching adorable cat videos on your cell phones. I bet none of you even know Dakota turned 21 just last week, China has seven kids that she knows of, Jason has a forty-year-old "ex" girlfriend..." Wheels paused, exhausted. He continued, slurring angrily, "I'm a better psychiatrist than you. Hell, Jack's a better shrink than you."

"Let's leave Jack out of this. He just tried to commit suicide..."

"What the hell is wrong with you, Stephanie? You just violated HIPAA laws. You can't disclose Jack's medical condition without his consent."

"You think you are smarter than me, Derrick?"

"Oh, Steph. First off, it's 'I am'. Smarter than I am. Self-evident. Secondly, quiz me if you must. You pick the subject." Wheels' slur continued to worsen.

"I'm going to have to ask you to leave if you continue your disruptive behavior, Derrick. Others would like to participate in group."

The group collectively shook their heads no. Being called a loser might be disagreeable, but given the overall perspective, not entirely unfaithful nor tiresome and, frankly, somewhat entertaining.

"Right there. That's the problem. You can't handle the truth. This place..." Wheels circled his hands... "Hell, the entire medical community, big pharma, the government, the mob, the cartels, the gangs...they are all in it together. It's one giant conspiracy. One giant circle jerk to screw the little guy. You're not here to heal us. You're here to make money off us and you have the full backing of the US government. Open your fucking..."

Wheels started jerking uncontrollably and foaming from his mouth. Stephanie stood, mouth agape. Jack took charge and yelled a series of commands in a loud, clear voice. "You, with the black hair and blue mock, call 911. You, with the blue stilettos and short skirt, start CPR. You, short lady with nose ring and pink hair, get a pillow. You, tall, African-American man, get me a cold beer."

CHAPTER EIGHTEEN
Barnes and Noble's SAC Meeting

Barnes and Noble were debating protocol with the Orlando FBI SAC. "Who's gonna remember we got a warrant when we get the bust?" Barnes insisted.

The SAC threw two jackets at Barnes. They were the files of the owner whose house he wanted to use as a surveillance house. "Nothing looks quirky here. I've got a public file that is clean on this guy and another that is almost completely redacted, even at my level of clearance."

"So he's some drug lord's accountant in witness protection. What do I care?"

"One, you don't know that. Two, you could get him killed."

Noble spoke up. "In all fairness, wouldn't we be doing him a solid? He did try to kill himself."

The SAC scoffed. "Not sure getting your skin peeled off and fed to yourself is considered a solid in most civilized circles."

"You say potato…"

"Do you want out of Orlando or not?" Noble asked.

"Look," the SAC continued to explain. "No self-respecting judge is going to grant you access to Jack's home without his permission. I sure as hell don't want part of any self-cannibalization torture on my watch. So here is a radical thought: how about you follow protocol for once in your career and go get his permission?"

Barnes turned to Noble. "Oh, jeez…why did we not think of that?" Barnes banged his head with the palm of his hand.

"I dunno, maybe because we are not sure if this Jack fellow is a rat?" Noble replied.

"You dead sit on his house? Then it's a chance you are going to have to take. We can keep him locked up for a few extra days there and monitor his calls from the joint directly. They don't get visitors or have cell phones. It'll be tough to contact anyone, even if he wanted to. Thank China, Trump, Fauci, nature, or whatever for Covid. Makes our job so much easier."

"Thank you for the lab leak to boost your investments in biological war…I mean, viral research and pharmaceuticals, Fauci," Noble prayed as instructed.

CHAPTER NINETEEN
Closed Bar

One Eye banged on the locked door of Foul Balls. It was late afternoon, he thought, why the hell is the bar closed? Bank opened the door. The bar was dark and empty inside with the exception of Bank and Purdue. "You make a cute nurse, Bilbo. Hell, I'd do you," One Eye quipped.

"It's Doctor Bilbo to you and I would bite off that syphilitic cock before I would let you poke it in me, you half-wit," Purdue retorted.

"You two can take it to the head later and work it out. For now, what we got on the product?" Bank asked.

"Like I was saying, nobody's talking at the hospital. Got a live one in the Loony Bin we can chat with, but that place is locked down tighter than the hospital," One Eye reported, omitting the insignificant details of the encounter.

"You find the bartender Earl?" Bank asked One Eye.

"Yeah. I don't think he ratted us out. He did give me a name of a junkie that was asking about us. A fellow name Horace. He was pointing at us the day we dropped off the bikes."

"I remember him. Meth head. Left before us."

"I haven't been able to find him yet, but I'm betting he is our man."

"Damn." Bank shook his head. "Running out of time. Where are the bartenders? Need to open up?"

One Eye looked at Bank, winked, and cocked his head.

"Both of 'em? Damn." Bank shook his head but knew it was of little use to scold One Eye. Accept the things you cannot change his therapist once told him. "Guess you're calling the boss and bartending 'til he can get someone else here. Doctor Bilbo, we are headed to the Bin to see a lady about a horse."

CHAPTER TWENTY
Bin Chaos, SNAFU

The Outlaw duo pulled under The Pines portico fortuitously just behind Barnes and Noble's arrival. The agents had changed into standard agent street clothing, but Bank recognized the two and grabbed Purdue before he stepped out of the truck. The original plan was for Purdue, aka Dr. Bilbo, to "admit" Bank as a ploy to gain access to the ward and, subsequently, to China. Bank was well known to the agents. Purdue had shaved, cut his hair, covered his tats, and was wearing a doctor's costume. He could still pass as a civilian. "Let's see how this plays out," Bank said.

Barnes was in a foul mood. The Outlaws had gone rouge and needed to return to the fold or feel the consequences. He yanked forcibly on the locked outer door. The receptionist barely looked up. Welcome to The Pines. He knocked. She answered an imaginary phone call. He placed his FBI credentials on the glass and knocked with the butt of his service weapon. The receptionist turned in her seat and continued to ghost chat on the phone. Noble pulled her service weapon and fired three times into the glass. The receptionist pushed a panic button, notifying the local police of an emergency, and simultaneously locking down the building. Barnes pulled on the second locked door. Noble fired again. The receptionist ducked behind the desk. Bank smiled. "You gotta admire their style."

"You gonna open that door?" Noble pointed at the door leading to the wards. "Or am I gonna have to shoot it, as well?"

"Ma'am, I hit the lock down button. I can't open anything until management and the police give the all-clear." Nobles shrugged and fired her service weapon into the glass, the sound of which reverberated down the hall like a circus cannon expelling a clown in the confines of a Harry Potter closet.

Bank looked at Purdue. "Your cue. Go find China."

Barnes and Noble strolled down the hallway yelling, "Jack, we are looking for Jack. Anyone know Jack? Jack?" It was surreal, as if two mad people had escaped into the asylum.

"What's Jack's last name? That might help," Barnes said to Noble.

Noble thumbed through Jack's jacket. "Smith. You got to be kidding me. No one has any frigging imagination anymore?" They came to ward 3, which was also locked, but at the intersection of the nurses' station. They bounded over the nurses' station counter and into the ward. A sign on the wall listed room 3B as belonging to one Jack S. The two strolled down the corridor, peering into each room as they passed, like creepy yokels peeking under the tent at a circus freak show until they arrived at 3B.

"Jack. You are a hard man to find." Barnes extended his hand. Jack was lying on the bed reading a Dorsey novel. Jack laughed out loud at one of the particularly inventive murderous passages from the book but did not look up or accept Barnes' outreached hand.

Noble pulled out her credentials. Jack glanced over at her badge and giggled. "Fancy that. I had one just like that in the 10th grade. Federal Body Inspector. Got mine in Panama City Beach. Didn't get me laid, though. Got a few drinks thrown in my face, so totally worth it. How about yours?"

Barnes was not surprised by Jack's reaction given his file. It was clearly not his first interaction with 'the man'. "Seems you may have some pent-up animosity toward law enforcement types, but we don't have a lot of time, so I'm gonna be brief. We need to borrow your house for a few days while you are inside the loony bin. Not to worry, Noble here will clean your place up spic and span when we leave, and you will never know we were there."

"Screw you, Neanderthal. I look like a maid to you?"

Jack, holding up a finger, interjected. "Housekeeper. I have been educated that 'maid' is now considered derogatory. Same job, different nomenclature, nothing else changes except the vernacular. 'Housekeeper'. Keep it woke. It's 2021. Feelings matter and words are like hand grenades."

Barnes scoffed and continued. "So, long story short, John Hancock here and we will be out of your figurative hair." Barnes presented the legal papers and offered Jack a pen. Jack refused the offered pen.

Nobles pulled her service weapon and placed it against Jack's temple. Jack scoffed. "Whoa, 'figurative hair', man. Ouch! Didn't we just talk about words are like hand grenades?"

"Stop the bullshit, Jack. Like he said. We are in a bit of a hurry. Your signature or your brains on the paper in 30 seconds. Dealer's choice."

Jack offered a half-crooked smile. "You know why I am in here, right?"

"You think I give a rat's ass, old man? Just sign."

"Might wanna do your research before you threaten me with a good time, lady."

"What makes you think I'm a lady, old man?"

"And now you're woke? Decades of misogynist Boomer programming that equate vaginas and boobs, no matter how tiny…" Jack squinted, tilted his head, and motioned at Noble's breasts, "…to the female sex".

Meanwhile, Purdue remained unmolested while following the agents' trail of chaos into the ward. He located China in the day room, salvaging snacks abandoned in the bedlam. Purdue took a seat beside her. "China?"

China snarled and gave him the once over. "Who asking, 'cause you sure as shit don't look like no hobbit or no doctor. And I ain't sharing my snacks, bitch."

"Got me. I'm gonna cut the bullshit and shoot straight with you. I'm looking for some missing product that I think you might can help me find." He handed her a $100 bill.

"You do speak my language. You got another one of those?"

"I do. You got something to offer me?"

China correctly read the room. "I just might. Your missing product uncut horse?"

"It is."

"You done this before, cracker? This is where you show me another President Hamilton."

Purdue chose to save time and forgo a history lesson, handing her a second $100 bill. "Hope you got more. This here China from Nordstrom's, not that hillbilly's Walmart or woke ass soccer mom's Bed, Bath, and Beyond with a 20-percent off coupon."

"I do. And I hope you got more information, but we got to move this conversation along. Expecting unwelcome company shortly."

"Do tell. All that shooting and shit...we call that Thursday in the hood. Fucking white privilege."

Purdue gave China a courtesy laugh and tilted his head. "Please continue."

"I was partying with a cracker meth head named Horace in a trailer park off Highway 411...no wait...441, yeah that be it. He had a garbage bag of pure horse that damn near killed me. No idea where he got it from."

"Where is Horace now?"

"The cops carted his retarded cracker ass and the horse to jail when they took me to the hospital."

"You remember the cops?" Purdue asked. He already knew that no cops had reported that large of a bust. Swede would have picked it up online and it would have been all over the news. The logical assumption was the cops lifted the heroin and murdered Horace.

"Nah, man." China briefly paused. "Wait a minute. You got another dead president?"

Purdue produced another dead secretary of treasury but tore it in half. "Make it good."

"One cop was white, middle-aged, normal cracker cop. Don't know his name. Other cop was a rookie. Good looking Hispanic fellow go by the name of Jesus. I'd do him. And I know what you are thinking. They lifted your shit, but not these cops. And I know cops. They were straight."

The sirens grew louder. Purdue gave China the other half of the bill and kissed her on the cheek. "Be blessed, China."

"You got a few minutes. I might find a way to refund a hundy," China said hungrily.

"Another time, darling. In a bit of a hurry," he said out loud. "That woman screw a lesser man to death," he smartly said to himself. Purdue made his way back the way he came, making room for the on-rushing police officers and EMTs. "Thank you for your service." He paused and saluted each and every one of them.

Noble pistol-whipped Jack. Jack picked up the pen, wiping blood from his eyes before clearly signing the document "Shrimp Johnson". Noble seethed, "tough guy," and hit Jack again with the butt of the pistol, knocking him unconscious. The agents fled, shooting their way out the back exit without checking the signature.

CHAPTER TWENTY-ONE
Jesus Saves

Bank called Swede to see what he could uncover about China and Horace's arresting police officers. In frustration, Bank tossed the burner phone at a Prius at a stoplight. The hipster driver foolishly shot Bank an aggressive bird. Bank smiled broadly. The Prius driver accelerated into traffic, broadsiding a city bus, scuffing the "Opioids Kill" signage imprinted on the side. The bus driver, high on oxy, continued on, oblivious of the collision. Bank blew the bloodied Prius driver a kiss as Bank drove by and motioned for the driver to call him.

Bank's working theory, despite China's assessment, was that the cops pinched the heroin. Bank subscribed to the theory of Occam's Razor; the simplest explanation is usually the correct one. Back at Foul Balls, One Eye was still tending bar. Bank and Purdue joined him awaiting news from Swede. Purdue went to the trailer, changed clothes, and grabbed another burner phone. Bank promoted one of the waitresses to bartender after asking her to perform a series of third grade arithmetic problems and photographing her driver's license. "Two rules. Don't steal. Don't snitch. We clear?"

She nodded yes.

"Gonna need you to say the words..." Bank lifted her name tag from her blouse. "... Dorothy."

"Yes, sir, Mr. Bank. I won't let you down."

"I highly doubt that. Just don't steal, don't snitch. Two simple rules. And giving away drinks is stealing..."

"Got it." She turned and walked to the bar.

"You know she missed half those math problems, right?" One Eye remarked.

"Here's to hoping her mistakes balance out 'cause the other two missed them all."

"And she did have the best tits."

Bank nodded. Purdue walked back in. "Got Swede for you." He handed Bank the phone. Bank walked outside.

After a few minutes, Bank returned. "Let's roll. We'll take the truck so I can fill you in."

Swede had found a record of Horace's arrest but not his booking, giving partial credence to Bank's theory that the cop's stole the heroin and killed Horace. No heroin was booked into the evidence room, but some was mentioned in the dispatch logs associated with Horace's arrest, dispelling Bank's theory. Why would the cops mention the heroin or Horace if they planned to steal the heroin? Nothing made sense. And where was Horace? They had the arresting officers' names and addresses. First stop was officer Eugene's home.

The Outlaws rolled up on Eugene's house and parked in his driveway. A "for sale" sign was placed prominently in his yard with a picture of a pretty little

blond taken 20 years prior and photo-shopped. She
was a solid ten. It was always a shock the first time
one met a real estate broker in person after seeing an
advertisement. "Where is your hot daughter?" No
lights were on inside. Bank rang the doorbell and
peeked inside to find the house empty. He sent Purdue
around back to double check.

The Outlaws found Jesus at home serving a 30-day
suspension for his part in the Gaia sexual harassment
incident. Jesus was rightfully indignant over the event
and eager to share his rage with anyone who would
listen other than the liberal press. Not many others
dared or cared. Always believe the woman was the new
mantra. Even listening to the man could get you labeled
as a misogynist or worse. It's as if some women have
forgotten they have fathers, brothers, and sons and that
not all women have well-intended motives. The old
saying, "Hell has no fury like a woman scorned," is not
woke, but has a taste of truth. Bank told One Eye to stay
put in the truck. He did not blend well with civilians,
much less cops. Bank and Purdue rang the doorbell. It
was agreed Purdue, freshly groomed, would take the
lead.

Jesus answered the door six tequilas deep. "If you
mother fuckers are with the press, get the fuck off my
porch."

"We look like reporters? We were just driving by
and saw your sweet ride in the driveway." Purdue
improvised. He was a salesperson by trade. First, find
common ground and make a connection. Then, make
the sale. There was a '67 Camaro SS with a sweet custom
paint job in the driveway. "For sale, by any chance?"

"No, man. That's my baby and I would sell my literal
baby if I had one before I would sell her. Restored her
from scratch. Got some pictures. Wanna see 'em?"

"Sure, man." They were in.

"Come on in. Wanna drink?"

"Yeah. Whatever you are having. So, why the press after you?"

"You don't know who I am?" Jesus poured them a shot of off-brand tequila, leaving the bottle on the table.

"Sorry, man, no. You a famous rigatoni singer or something?"

Jesus laughed. "I'm Jesus, the cop's partner that arrested that naked feral bitch." Jesus showed them the videos.

Bank noticed it first. "That's some crazy shit, man. Why you driving a beat up morgue van?"

"Rough day, man." Jesus explained getting shot up by the farmer and having to trade cars.

"Were you guys coming from another call or something when you got shot up?" Bank asked.

Jesus threw back a shot. His face grimaced. "Shit." He grabbed his keys and went running out of the house. Purdue grabbed him. "You can't drive, man! What is it?"

"Horace. We left Horace in the back of the patrol car."

Bank and Purdue exchanged anxious glances. "Where is the car?"

"Guessing still at the impound lot?"

"We will drive you, man. Hop in the truck."

Bank was needlessly worried that Jesus was drunk, out of uniform, and on probation when they pulled up to the police impound lot. The attendant was a Hispanic man known to Jesus. They embraced. "That some bullshit you got suspended, bro. What kind of world we live in when you can't even grope a little white tit. These Bastards need to head down to any old border town for the day."

"You telling me. And it weren't even me that grabbed her tiny little tits. It was Emmitt. He had to leave town. The pussy hat protesters were blasting Alanis Morrissette music in the middle of night right outside his window."

"Alanis who?"

"Shit, I don't know. Something about a Jagged Pill and hating on men."

"But Emmitt? That's a crying shame. He's the nicest cracker pig I ever met. He bring me burritos every time he come by, ask about mi familia, he even know me in the grocery tienda, hombre."

"Can we move the tearful reunion along? We kinda on a tight schedule," Bank requested.

Jesus smirked but asked the attendant, "Where my cruiser parked? I need to get some personal belongings out of it".

"Let me check." The attendant went inside the shack, returning shortly with the keys and the lot number for the car.

"Thanks, bro. Another favor. Can you kill the cameras? I'm on probation. Might get us both in a spot of trouble if they see me here," Jesus explained.

Bank and Purdue looked at each other like Christmas had arrived early. One Eye sat quietly in the truck out of sight. He literally had criminal element written on his face. Fortunately, Jesus was too drunk to notice.

"No problem, hermano." He pointed at the camera currently videoing them. "I'll take care of this, too."

Bank spoke up. "Gracias. We'll bring you back some Tacos and Dos XX."

The attendant looked at Bank. "Seriously, man? That's some fucked up racist shit right there. I am gonna report that shit to Joe Biden." Bank was speechless. For a moment. Even Outlaws have feelings. Well, Bank did.

"Just fucking with you, cabron. But can you make it burritos and go easy on the beans. My ol' lady bitch about me farting in bed. Y no mi quiero Taco Bell. There's a Chinese street vendor named Gao that sells the best authentic Mexican food in Ocala. Entiendo, cabron?"

"Yeah, tacos from Taco Bell, extra beans."

They made short work of finding the cruiser. Jesus jumped out of the truck and found Horace unresponsive in the back seat. He fumbled with the keys. Bank took them from him and opened the car door. A foul smell poured from inside the car like a tsunami of rancid human waste, which was more literal than metaphor. Bank checked Horace's pulse. It was faint, but he was alive. Jesus pulled out his cell to call 911.

"Are you nuts?" Bank asked. "You will go to jail."

"But he might die."

"He'll die for sure. We will all die someday. And truthfully, if this washout dies, the world will be a better place. We will drop you home and take him to the hospital, so you are completely divorced from the situation." Jesus reluctantly nodded his head yes. Horace wasn't worth losing his career over, much less going to jail. "Now help Purdue get him in the back of the truck."

While they were busy depositing Horace in the truck, Bank opened the trunk and retrieved the heroin. It appeared light. Jesus turned and saw Bank with the bag and his face scrunched up in suspicion. "How did you know about that?" Purdue hit him over the head with his gun. They propped Jesus up in the backseat of the truck, wiped the blood from his face, and headed back to the house of Jesus.

There, Bank called 911. Jesus was still unconscious. "You didn't have to bash his brains in." Never good to kill a cop. And Jesus seemed like a nice enough guy.

"One minute, you guys bitch I'm not tough enough, the next…"

"Is it your time of the month, honey? Let's go find Gao."

"Fuck you."

"You would like that."

"Maybe, but dibs for top."

Gao was just a few blocks from the impound lot in a predominantly working-class, Hispanic neighborhood lined with small cafes, tiendas, bars, and punctuated with whore houses frequented by gringo tourists seeking relief from the dark magic that was Orlando. He was easy to spot as he was the only 10-year-old Chinese kid on the block. Gao was straight from an Indiana Jones movie or a Dr. Suess' kid's book. He had jet black hair with bangs and a considerable gap between his front teeth. Sometimes you just draw them like you see them with no ill intent. Bank ordered four burritos, no beans, a water, and two Dos XX from Gao. Gao gave Bank the gringo discount and charged him double the amount, $15. Bank gave him a $20 and said, "Keep the change, cabron". Bank assumed cabron was a term of endearment.

"Fuck off, gringo cracker." Gao was being a bit redundant, but his Tiger mom had said white people were a bit weak-minded. Compared to Gao, who would later graduate with honors from MIT, his mom was not far off the mark.

"You little shit."

Bank turned to kick his ass. Purdue grabbed his arm. "Let's stay on mission." Bank poured some of the water in Horace's mouth and left the rest in the back of the truck. They returned to the lot and gave the attendant the burritos and keys. "Gracias, cabrons. Donde mi amigo, Jesus?"

"No hablo Espanol, Senor."

"Where Is Jesus?"

"In my heart." Bank placed his hands theatrically over his heart. Horace woke up in the back of the truck and started banging around.

"What the fuck was that?" the lot attendant asked.

"Mi perros. Enjoy the burritos. Adios, cabron." Bank and Purdue sped off, less the attendant's curiosity peek and create a tertiary problem for the duo.

CHAPTER TWENTY-TWO
Reverend Mack and Doctor Jacob

Jack returned from the hospital after an overnight stay for observation for a concussion with 15 stitches across the crown of his head and a black eye. A babysitter was unavailable on short notice, so Jack was restrained like a common criminal. He resembled a jealous boyfriend on a Sunday morning after a night of heavy partying at the local dance club with a girlfriend two paygrades beyond his reach. Fresh meat for drunk predators. The nurse said it added character. Jack said it gave him a headache, and the $15,000 bill for the multitude of "required" tests gave him a bad attitude. "They charged me $517 to stick a plastic tube up my dick? I can piss just fine on my own." Jack was tempted to display his urination prowess but decided the demonstration might secure him more time in the Bin. The $350 for the restraints was simply above the pail.

"And 53 cents," the nurse dryly replied, handing back his bill. "Can I help you with anything else?"

"Yeah, what are these charges for a respiratory therapist, occupational therapist, speech therapist, child psychiatrist, and OBGYN?" Jack asked.

"You saw them while you were in surgery. Anything else I can help you with?" the nurse offered.

Jack sighed in defeat.

∞∞∞∞

The shattered windows at the Bin had been boarded up, the glass swept mostly clear, and the bullet holes patched but not yet painted. Jack found the day room was packed on his arrival. Stephanie had called a muster of the inmates to provide emotional counseling for the "unfortunate event of the previous day."

Wheels slurred more than normal, barely able to lift his head from the increased sedative dosage. "You mean...the fucking shoot out at the OK Bin." He forced a feeble laugh.

Stephanie made a note to further increase Wheels' dosage. "First, this is The Pines, not the Bin." She was interrupted with a chorus of laughter. She self-soothed by tugging on her mini skirt and smoothing her size smedium blouse, regaining her composure as the laughter subsided. "Second, no reason for hyperbole. No one was injured."

Wheels fought through the fog and laughed maniacally. "Turn around, Steph. Jack looks like he was on the losing end of a bar fight."

Jack waved. "You should see the other guy...not a mark on him."

"An unrelated injury," Stephanie assured the group. "He was not shot."

"What, then, Jack go all ninja and escape the Bin to visit a BDSM sex club and accidently pick from the supersized menu or did he just forget his safe word?" Wheels asked. He shuttered, rattling the wheelchair.

China laughed. "Cracker pussy. Gotta learn to take it up the ass or fight if you gonna keep hanging in the joint."

Wheels motioned toward Jason curled into a fetal position not much larger than a dusty cheese wheel at a convivence store check-out counter. "Nothing, Steph?" Wheels asked in disgust. "You are less than worthless."

"For all we know, Jack's injuries were self-inflicted. You know he was…"

"Jesus Christ, God almighty. I got it from here, Steph." Reverend Mack took Steph's arm and escorted her out of the room. Mack was a very large black man who grew up in the projects and, with his upbringing, had witnessed the dark underbelly of society. Mack was a bit of a stereotype. Raised by his grandmother, he joined a gang and did a few years in juvie. Mack found football or, rather, football found Mack. He was big and aggressive. A high school coach pulled some strings and got Mack transferred to his school where Mack excelled at sports and found he had a knack for academics, as well.

Mack was highly recruited and made first string all-American his sophomore year as a linebacker at Florida. In his junior year, his knee was crushed on crack back block and his football career ended the same week his grandmother died. Mack was still in the hospital and unable to attend her funeral. The university, in a common act of greed, dropped his scholarship, and Mack was forced to drop out of school and return to the projects. Predictably, Mack was bitter and turned to drugs and alcohol to cope. Eventually, he was evicted from the projects and ended up living on the streets.

∞∞∞∞

Years earlier…

A police dispatcher routed Emmitt to a disturbance in a 7-11 parking lot near Zombieland. "Damn," Earl muttered. He was relatively new to the force and his partner was out. A group of teenage skateboarders were harassing a large, black, homeless man. Earl sounded his siren and lit up his lights and skateboarders scurried into the darkness. Earl sat down and threw the bag, subsequently shattering the empty bottle. "Mack is that you?" Emmitt asked.

"Who the hell asking?"

"Emmitt. We played high school football together."

Mack shielded his eyes from the light. "I'll be torch juggling with Klansman at a Trump rally. Never would have seen that coming. You a damn cop now, Emmitt? Thought you were a jarhead."

"Got tired of getting shot at."

"And what you do now? You never was the brightest bulb." Mack and Emmitt laughed. "Buy me a drink for old times' sake."

"How about a nice meal and cup of coffee?"

"Drink sounds better, but that'll do in a pinch."

After dinner, a pot of coffee, and some catching up on old times, Emmitt brought Mack to his house and set Mack up in the guest bedroom. Mack had done some awful things in his life, but, for the most part, to awful people. He felt like a burden to Emmitt and his family, and they were anything but awful. Mack quickly sobered up and moved into a Christian homeless shelter. There he found Jesus; just maybe not the one most profess to hold in their hearts. And, with Jesus, a purpose in life.

∞∞∞∞

The inmates knew Mack's story. He was kind, humble, charismatic, spoke softly, and carried the kind of gravitas that can only be earned. When Earl entered a room, he owned it. Not even Wheels challenged Mack.

"What happened to you, Jack?" Mack asked softly. Mack had learned that whispered words roar.

"Apparently, as Wheels sees it, I forgot my safe word."

Mack chuckled. "I gonna call bullshit on that, Jack. I take you more as a missionary style, lights off, socks on kind of guy more so than that kinky stuff." China laughed. "And you, China, I don't even want to conjure on your sexual predilections." Mack turned back to Jack. "Did anyone call the police?"

"First off, I do take my socks off. And yes, I do turn the lights off as a matter of courtesy to my partner. Secondly, you see, Mack, it was the police." Mack nodded. "That tracks." Mack knew something was up with Jack but could not yet put all the pieces together. "You good, brother?"

"As soon as I get out of this hellhole." Mack took no offense. In fact, he agreed. He was not an employee but a volunteer. His real job was more audacious.

Mack turned his attention to Jason. "What up with you, little man?"

Jason drooled and mumbled something unintelligible. China laughed. Mack's brow wrinkled as he locked eyes with China. "Let's me and you go have some one-on-one time."

"Best you not forget your safe word, Reverend," Jack warned.

Steph reclaimed the meeting. "Can I be of more assistance to anyone else?"

Wheels laughed but refrained from employing a witty retort.

Jack spoke up. "Yeah, Steph. My 72-hour Backer Act jail sentence expires sometime today and I have yet to even see the prison warden. Isn't the warden required to give me a once over 'fore I get my walking papers?" Jack asked.

She awkwardly laughed. Jack wasn't being funny.

"You have not seen a psychiatrist since you have been here, Jack?"

"No, Ma'am."

"I'll let him know. And don't call me ma'am. You're old enough to be my granddad."

"That's your line? Don't flatter yourself, Steph. If you're not fifty, you damn sure been rode hard and put up wet. And, if you rather, I have a few other less pleasant greetings I could use."

Jack started to list off several expletives, but Wheels interjected. "Oh please, don't even get me started."

"Nurse works just fine."

"Nurse?" Wheels and Jack exclaimed in unison, giggling uncontrollably like toddlers being tickled by their mothers.

"Just curious, Nurse Ratchet, you ever hear of this little law called false imprisonment?" Jack inquired once he gained his composure.

"I'm a nurse, Jack, not a lawyer." She lowered her voice to whisper. "But you were Baker Acted, Jack."

Jack looked at her wide-eyed. "First off, that's Mister Jack to you. Secondly, if I were you, I would request a refund from whatever online school gave you your nursing degree. And finally, no shit? And Baker Acted? Thank God. I thought I checked into this hellhole on my own volition. So, I am not crazy, after all. Imagine my relief. Thing is, the Baker Act expires after 72 hours. Tick tock, bitches." Jack retreated to his quarters.

After a brief spell, a very attractive, charming lady came by Jack's room. "Jack," she seductively whispered as she sat on his bed, uninvited. She inquired of his wounds while touching his arm and smiling coyly, never breaking eye contact. Jack was just old enough to know better. He was cat nip for the old biddies but was not a catch on his best day for younger women two letter grades below this one suggestively lounging on his bed. This not being his best day, he smelled a trap. "Jack," she said handing him a form he couldn't read. "Can you sign this paper for me so we can work on processing you out?"

"And what, might I inquire, is this form?" Jack asked without even looking at the paper.

"One that gets the ball rolling for the team to begin to put a plan together to get a date to process you out."

Jack shook his head. "Sounds like government double speak for a discharge date other than right now."

"Yes." She hesitated.

"When does my 72 hours expire?"

"Technically, in about an hour, but the 18 hours you spent in the hospital doesn't count."

"That tracks. I damn near get murdered on your watch and get punished for it. Makes perfect sense. Can you read me the headline on the form? I can't read without my glasses." He caught an orchestrated glimpse of her nipples as she leaned over. The day was not totally lost.

She read the headline, sheepishly. "Self-Committal Form."

Jack looked up at her, seething, nice nipples forgotten. "Get the hell out of my room."

"But Jack…" She produced another form. "You already signed one."

Jack scoffed and took a cursory look at the form. "I know Hillary has taken a bad turn, yet even so. I ain't her. And do I look like somebody who would fuck Bill? Not that I am sure she ever did either, but that's another story. Long story short, you ain't got shit."

About an hour later, the attractive aide returned, in a less seductive mood and with less visible cleavage. "Let's get you to the doctor, Jack. Follow me." Jack noted the trunk was as well-equipped as the hood. The shrink was a tall, thin, black man with a Jamaican accent. He introduced himself as Jacob.

Angrily, he started the conversation. "You owe Betty an apology." Jack stared at Jacob incredulously without saying a word. "Nothing to say, Jack?"

Jack surmised the shapely young aide and the shrink might have more than a strict hands off business relationship. Jack spoke in a whisper, forcing Jacob to strain to hear him. "I got plenty to say. Very little you are going to want hear." Jack tilted his head down, showing his still bloodied head.

Jacob regathered. "Let's start anew. I am here to help. Tell me about why you are so angry and tried to end your life."

"I had rather have my wrinkly nut sack shaved with a dull razor by Michael J. Fox while live on the View than have a shrink in this hellhole try and psychoanalyze me."

Jacob nervously shifted in his chair. "Mocking the disabled is not acceptable behavior in polite society."

"My bad. I was unaware I was in the presence of polite society. Should we send the servants for tea and crumpets?"

A woman on the ward screamed a river of expletives only to be answered by a resounding chorus of, "Shut the fuck up, bitch". Jacob sat stoned-faced.

Jack smiled. "I'll have my tea with two sugars, please."

Jacob rubbed his forehead. He was accustomed to dealing with crazy but not crazy, smart, and seemingly fearless.

"First, what are you, Jacob? Doctor, psychologist, camp counselor, pedo priest, janitor...I kinda prefer janitor, frankly. Janitors tend to have more integrity, work ethic, and don't diddle their under-age charges. I can relate to janitors."

"I'm sorry you feel that way, Jack."

Jack sighed. "If only contrition assuaged guilt, Jacob."

Jacob scoffed. "I'm a healer, a psychiatrist. We do God's work here."

Jack rolled with genuine laughter. He thought Jacob might actually believe himself, which, into itself was frighteningly ignorant. "I am sorry for your unfortunate career choice, but okay. I'll give you the benefit of the doubt that you think because of your expensive education you are a healer. Let's keep those lobotomies in the back of your brain, though...or, should I say, front? But do I trust you? No. Do I trust this place? Hell, no. Do I trust the health care system? Hell, no. You are a for-profit system. Regardless of your bullshit published mission statement for public consumption, it is your primary mission to maximize shareholder profits. To do so, you need to maximize bed occupancy. Holding patients against their will is a great tactic to do just that, no? And over-prescribing expensive drugs is yet another method with an added bonus of keeping the inmates sedated and your job much easier. And don't even get me started on God's work or we will be here all day."

"You accusing this hospital of malpractice?"

"What was her name...Nice tits, spacious trunk, pretty smile...oh yeah, Betty, yeah, I think the shoe fits, Jacob, and some of God's better work, I might add."

"That is a serious charge, Jack. Not to mention sexual harassment."

"For the love of God, Jacob. Are you blind or stupid? If anyone was sexually harassed, it was me in order to coerce me into signing my execution papers by distracting an old fart with a great set of unleashed tits and a nice ass. But I am glad you're paying attention. I know I was. Gonna add another serious charge Jacob: false imprisonment."

"You were Baker Acted, Jack. Comes with the package."

"That bullshit play clock is about to expire."

"Why do you think it is bullshit? You tried to take your own life, Jack. Do you deny this?"

"Why should it matter if I did? I just don't see where the state has a say in what I do with my body. Everyone should have the right to choose their own fate, even if that fate is death. Case in point. Let's go down the abortion rabbit hole for a jiffy without judging abortion on its merits. Tearing apart a living fetus...or whatever we want to call the living organism in the womb waiting to be born, to absolve our guilt, is not only legal, but also virtually celebrated in this country. I hear Biden is considering making Margaret Sanger's birthday a national holiday. Maybe rename the Washington Monument Sanger's Phallic. I think the progressives have agreed to overlook her views on eugenics for the greater good. A woman's right to choose what she does with her own body, right? To hell with the rights of that life inside of her. Okay, maybe I judged a little. Hey, maybe we should make abortion legal to the age of 18. I might could get behind that idea. Yet, let a retired 60-year-old man try to take his own life without harming another living creature and he is locked up? In what universe does that make sense? So yes, I am angry at the hypocrisy. The sheer lunacy of locking anyone up in a shit-gilded prison like The Pines for their "own good" is the zenith of ignorance and akin to capturing a killer whale and imprisoning it in a fish tank for their own safety. The Pines is a carnival freak show on acid where the audience grinds the organ while the monkey flings shit at the patients and ejaculates on the nurses with his finger knuckles deep in his nose."

Jacob scribbled rapidly. "That's some pretty powerful imagery," he responded.

"They gave me some good drugs at the real hospital. Besides. I am in the loony bin, after all. Play the part you are assigned. I'm a method actor. Total immersion in the role."

Jacob sighed. "Also, Jack, you don't seem to respect the rights for a woman to choose."

"Murder a choice? That's the party line? Again, not judging, just asking. I have several people on my kill list if it is a choice. But I do see you paid attention in your mandatory women's studies class. Did well in your gender studies, and white privilege classes, too, I bet. China, the country, well the inmate as well, is so going to kick our asses. Seriously Jacob, you are a smart dude, but you drank the Kool-Aid, man. Sack up and Sapere Aude, dude. Challenge the inconvenient truth. Don't be a sheep. Read you some Kant. I just want equal rights, Jacob. Seems fair. So when do I get out of here?"

"Humor me first, Jack, if you will. I need to feel like I at least tried to earn my money and, at a minimum, scribble some notes in your file. Can you do that for me, Jack?"

Jack nodded yes.

"Why would one consider suicide?"

"Seems self-evident, Jacob…wanting to die."

Jacob scoffed. "So hypothetically, if you did attempt suicide, what would have been the last thing going through your mind before you committed the act?"

Jack was no singer. In fact, auto tune even returned an error message at his attempts. But, for some reason, he started belting out:

> "T'was grace that taught my heart to fear
> And grace my fear relieved
> How precious did that grace appear
> The hour I first believed."

His singing was greeted with a chorus of yelled "shut the fuck up" from the ward.

"Did I hear encore?" Jack shouted back.

"Only if you want me to tear out your vocal cords and shove them up Jason's ass," China replied.

"I'll take that as a maybe and we will revisit later," Jack shouted.

"How about I cut your wee dick off with a plastic spoon and use it to floss your teeth?" China replied.

"Okay. Hard pass, then."

Jacob was furiously scribbling in his notepad throughout the exchange but neither he nor any of the staff made any effort to intervene. "Jack, can we get back on track now?"

"I thought I was giving you some pretty primo material for your notes and memoir."

Jacob scoffed. "Amazing Grace, Jack. Why so? Are you a believer?"

"In the all-powerful, all-just, all-knowing God?"

"Yes, Jack, that one."

"Nope."

"Can I ask why not?"

"Yes."

Jacob sighed, "Okay then, why do you not believe in that God?"

"Heard this on some movie one day. Two old Holocaust survivors arguing which of their concentration camps was more hellish than the other. One suggested only God can answer that. The second responded, how would He know. He was not there."

"I don't get it." Jacob responded.

Jack shook his head. "Jacob, how could an all-knowing, all-powerful, all-just God allow the suffering of innocents?"

"Most priests say original sin, Jack."

"Such bullshit. Me, you, most adults...yeah, we sinned and probably deserve our comeuppance. But children, babies...Nah, I don't believe in that, dude."

Jacob scribbled furiously.

Jack paused and bowed his head before speaking in a whisper. "As I sat by mother's death bed watching her suffer, it was the song playing when she asked me to kill her. That should be good enough to finish out your notes, Jacob. Now, when do I get out of this hellhole?"

Jacob ignored the question. "So, you are admitting you attempted suicide, Jack?"

"I am giving you a reason that I would take my own life but there are a few others more motivated in line ahead of me."

Jacob scribbled in his notebook.

"Adding paranoia to my diagnosis?"

"Jack, are you suggesting someone tried to kill you and staged your suicide?"

"I honestly don't know. Certainly considered suicide on a number of occasions. Gotta admit the world is pretty upside down right now, at least for us old farts. But frankly, I have no memory of that day. And here is where I'll put the shovel down. So once again Dr. Jacob, when do I get the hell out of here?"

"You are both a fascinating and aggravating subject that I truly believe needs counseling."

"Hard pass, Doc. You'll have to find another form of entertainment. But, if you like, I will send you a mixed tape of my greatest hits. You and Betty can listen to it between the sheets for motivation."

Jacob scoffed but did not rise to the taunt. He made a few more notes before shuffling through his files. Not normally one to give in to the quiet, Jack broke the silence by continuing with a warning. "But, Doc, since you seem to be different, albeit slightly, from the rest of the staff in that you actually believe you are in this to make a difference and not to exert power over the most vulnerable, I feel obligated to warn you. When, not if, but when I get out of here, I have numerous resources at my disposal that I plan to use once you have gotten comfortable and I am just a dim shadow in your rearview mirror...almost forgotten. I plan, just as Paris Hilton did with the Accountability for Congregate Care Act, to make it my sole purpose to ensure no other individual experiences the share torture mental health patients under your, and other like, facility offers hidden from the pretty marketing pamphlets you spew out. I promise a day of reckoning is coming and it will bring this vast profit-driven machine down. The systemwide lack of transparency and accountability will be brought down. Get ahead of the game and get out while you can."

"The normal stay here is three to five days." Jacob continued shuffling papers, stopping to study a couple, uttering quirky noises that Jack found disconcerting. "Your Baker Act got paused for your hospital stay for 18 hours." Shuffle, shuffle, shuffle. "Your meds were changed today which will add 48 hours for observation." Shuffle, shuffle, shuffle. A puzzled look crossed Jacob's face as he focused on a singular form. "This is peculiar. There is some strange, indefinite hold form in your file issued from the NSA I am not familiar with…" Jacob trailed off, visibly shaken as Jack's words replayed in Jacob's head as he attempted to hold the redacted copy up to a light to see if there were any words to be made out to no avail. Jacob recalled the shakeup of the youth shelter industry with no head safe from rolling and knew it was time to find a new line of work. This gig was up.

Jack bolted from Jacob's office and made a beeline to the phone. He bumped some new meat off the only phone in the ward. New Meat protested mildly until he remembered where he was and saw the crazed look in Jack's eyes. Jack dialed a number he had memorized 25 years ago and had not used in the last 10 years…his wife's.

CHAPTER TWENTY-THREE
Grilling Horace

Bank sent One Eye back to the safe house with the product recovered from the police cruiser to get it weighed, cut, and on the street while he and Purdue remained in Ocala to deal with Horace and resolve the whereabouts of the outstanding merchandise. Bank was certain the bag recovered from the police cruiser was light but would have to wait until One Eye called him to know just how much product was missing. Purdue dragged Horace from the truck and locked him in the trailer before going inside Foul Balls for some food, drinking water, and off-brand Clorox...Clorocks.

Meanwhile, Barnes and Noble activated their elite surveillance team to begin setting up Jack's home. Barnes, perpetually cantankerous, instructed the team that speed was of the essence and damage to the home was of no concern and, in fact, encouraged. The team arrived within the hour in a Total DisComfort box truck and two vans. One crew of the team began unloading the equipment in the garage. The other crew cleared out Jack's living room and dining room and began drilling holes in the walls and ceilings for cables. It was evident by the amount of unnecessary drilling and drywall damage there was no plan of operations. Ironically, all the extra equipment and personnel did require extra cooling. The FBI pulled strings, and, within an hour, a legitimate Total DisComfort truck pulled up and, working through the night, sloppily installed an additional 5-ton commercial air conditioning unit creating only slightly more damage than the surveillance team had inflicted on Jack's house. They were instructed not to be constrained by neatness, building codes, safety, nor long term reliability. The AC just needed to work for a week, irrespective of damage. This was Total DisComfort's area of expertise…damage, hidden or obvious. The five-man crew worked through the night with outdoor floodlighting and power tools to get the job done. Several neighbors called in noise complaints to the police that went unanswered…Bike Week and all. Choose your battles.

Ormond Beach and Daytona are small communities with a reliable grapevine and heavy usage of Nextdoor's social media platform. By noon the following day, the entire county knew the FBI had a surveillance house set up in Ormond Beach. Speculation was rampant, especially among the casserole widows and divorcees that had vied for Jack's unrequited attention. Which, based on the rabid Nextdoor responses, was well over 1,000 who knew Jack intimately or knew someone who knew someone who knew Jack and felt compelled to add "facts" to the conversation. One insisted Jack was a retired circus clown who fostered and ate small children in his basement. Given the high water table in the area, basements in Florida were called swamps. Others were a bit closer to the truth. But, then again, give a thousand monkeys a typewriter…

One Eye had yet to arrive, and the Outlaws were downing beers and fishing on the dock using hot dogs as bait. They had an unobstructed view of the activity in Jack's yard and drive. "Fish on, mother fuckers," one of the bikers hooted. His rod bent violently as he struggled to reel in the fish while smoking a cigarette and holding his beer. Apache took the lucky fisherman's beer and demonstrated how to pull the rod up and reel in while simultaneously lowering the rod. The biker had not fished since he was a kid and then only in small ponds where he mostly caught perch the size of his hand. Five minutes later, the biker reeled in a giant six-pound catfish. His excitement was palatable and contagious. It was like Santa had delivered the disabled orphan kid his entire Christmas wish list. The biker, in his excited state, reached barehanded to unhook the monster and received an unpleasant surprise. Saltwater catfish are outfitted with sharp, slimy spikes that inject a mild, but very painful, toxin. It won't kill you but, for a brief moment, one might prefer it had. Christmas at the orphanage was over. The biker released a stream of obscenities, catching the attention of the agents at the surveillance house.

Apache pointed at the agents with his beer and blew them a kiss. "Can't say if you or them mother fuckers are dumber. Gonna go call Bank. Meantime, quit yer whining. You been shot three times and didn't put on a community theater performance like that. Now sack up, get the hook out of that poor catfish, and get him back in the water."

Bank was puzzled by Apache's report. These two agents were not following the FBI playbook and that concerned him. He believed the surveillance house to be a diversion. Even so, it would be active. He called back to the house with a list of instructions. "Turn the music down, grab something to write with, and listen up. First, stop drinking." Bank knew that was a big ask, likely to be considered more as a guideline than a rule. He continued with his instructions. "Second, search each of your bikes methodically 'til you find the tracking device. When you find it, leave it there for now and don't ride that bike. Third, post two guards outside and one inside at all times. Fourth, don't talk business inside or outside. Fifth, point some speakers at their house and play loud, offensive…" Bank pondered for a moment. "Maybe some David Alan Coe music nonstop. Also, play it inside the house. That'll drive them woke ass commie FBI agents nuts. One Eye should be there shortly. Get to work and communicate business with him in writing. Then, burn the notes."

∞∞∞∞∞

Purdue fed and watered Horace from a safe distance. There was no reason to restrain him. Horace devoured the meal and asked for more. "I'll get you more. But first, let's get you cleaned up and have a chat. Strip."

Horace complied. Purdue motioned for him to move over by the building and face the wall.

"Brace yourself and close your eyes." Purdue sprayed Horace down with a hose. Purdue then poured half a bottle of bleach over Horace's head before thoroughly rinsing. Horace meekly protested but otherwise accepted his fate for the promise of another burger. Purdue repeated the process on the front side muttering,

"I don't know which one of us is getting the worst end of this". Naked Horace resembled a disturbingly well-endowed stick man dipped in molasses and rolled in hair balls.

Purdue had procured one of the waitress' after-work-party change of clothing, heroin kit, and a roll of paper towels. He reckoned Horace was down to a size six. He tossed them at Horace. "You can put these on in the trailer."

"But these are women's clothes. Shit, it's a mini skirt, a halter top, and a damn thong." Horace protested as if even a quark of dignity remained on the table.

"Better than them filthy rags you had on...and you damn sure better be wearing that thong, Horace. If I see your dick again, I will slice it off with a plastic knife covered in maggots." Purdue locked Horace in the trailer and went back inside to grab another bottle of water for Horace and a whiskey for himself. He needed to unsee the horrors he had beheld.

After three shots of Jack-ish, Purdue felt reinforced to face the disagreeable task at hand and returned to the trailer. The waitress's outfit fit loosely on Horace's emaciated frame. Horace went to sit. "For the love of baby Jesus, stand!" The Outlaws were fans of Talladega Nights. Horace complied. Purdue tossed him the water bottle. "Where is the rest of my heroin you jacked?"

"I ain't took your heroin, man. Do I look stupid?"

Purdue couldn't help but laugh. "In spades, Horace. We know you did. Just listen. Me and Bank here aren't like most of the Outlaws." He lied. Bank would give the order to have Horace killed in a heartbeat for sport. Purdue pondered Bank may even do it himself. "We are on the business side. We get our shit back without a lot of trouble and you are on your way without even much of an ass-kicking. In fact, I got a little parting gift for you…" Purdue pulled out the waitress's heroin kit and held it up to Horace. "If you make this easy, this too could be yours."

Horace was doing a bit of whimsical mental calculus. He had a lifetime of heroin under a trailer. The details of the exact location of said trailer were a bit fuzzy, but he was confident he would eventually locate the stash. This Purdue guy did not look that tough. He was not tied up and he could make a run for it. He was in a dress with no shoes. He had no money on him. Purdue was offering instant gratification. Making a run for it or cooperate with this guy?

Horace's stomach rumbled. The food service manager at Foul Balls reluctantly ordered the lowest grade of meat suitable for human consumption from its food supplier after having inquired if there was a cheaper grade available. Not having eaten in days, the greasy Foul Balls burger made an explosive, unsolicited exodus, and Horace promptly shit his thong. The thong's basic design was for style, not function, and held little of the foul mixture as it spilt onto the trailer floor like an erupting stool volcano that was transcendent in its nature to the two unfortunate witnesses. Multiple lava flows of shit dripped from the trailer onto the parking lot, forming new land masses of steaming poo.

"Mother of God!" Purdue screamed like a little girl that just saw her puppy squashed by the garbage truck.

"Can I get another burger? This time, with cheddar and a side of fries," Horace nonchalantly requested while wiping his face with a shit-covered hand.

Gagging, Purdue hosed off Horace and the trailer before locking him back up and returning to Foul Balls for a bowl of tomato soup, that was, in truth, microwaved, watered-down catsup squeezed from pinched fast food to-go packets, a bottle of water, and another whiskey for himself. On return to the trailer, he picked up a short length of pipe as his patience with Horace was spent. "Eat the soup and give up the heroin or get the pipe, princess craps-a-lot."

"This ain't no burger, dude. Where's my fries? And my skirt is all wet."

"First world problems, asshole. Stop dawdling. Eat the soup and talk."

Horace sipped the soup and spit it out. "This tastes like watered-down catsup."

"Well good to know you don't have Covid." Purdue was not vaccinated. He had less faith in big pharma than even the most devout anti-vaxxers. He'd rather take his less than 1 percent chance of dying from Covid than trust the vaccine that the government assured the public was safe. The government simultaneously protected the makers of the drug from any liability and hid the vaccine data for 75 years just in case it was not safe. Follow the money.

It only took one whack with the pipe to convince Horace that Purdue was serious. "It's under a derelict trailer in Zombieland. Now give me my kit."

"Product first, kit second. And you said 'a' trailer much like you lack total certainty as to the exact location of said trailer. And I am pretty sure 'derelict' doesn't narrow it down."

"I may be a bit fuzzy on the details, but nothing a little hit would not resolve."

Whack. "That help, Horace?"

"A bit. I know the park. Just not certain the precise trailer."

Whack.

"But if I see it, I'll know it. The dump even ain't got no door. LMAO," Horace deadpanned, finishing the soup.

"Okay, then. Let's roll, Mrs. Doubtfire. And keep your knees together and ankles crossed like a proper lady," Purdue said while gathering up a flashlight and the pipe from the trailer.

CHAPTER TWENTY-FOUR
Ezekiel

Mealtime at the Bin was frequently an adventure. In principle, the four wards were separated by propensity for violence and, more or less, level of crazy. At mealtimes, the wards inmates overlapped for a few minutes, creating a predilection for mayhem. As in the wild, predators in the Bin recognized easy prey. Jack had wisely cultivated a friendship with China, Wheels, and Dakota. China and Wheels had figurately kissed and made up, the science-denying wheelchair ride never consummated. China was explosive but Jack sensed he understood her triggers and bribed her with most of his food which was of no great sacrifice for Jack. The food sucked to any but the least discerning palate and was no more a sacrifice than forgoing a rectal exam provided by a fat-fingered doctor with Palsy and long fingernails. Yet China was the catfish of land mammals. Even some of the homeless inmates pined for more appetizing dumpster-diving cuisine. China held quantity above quality and held firm to her conviction in not working for food. Dumpster-diving, chicken wings and crab legs were work. Although, truth be told, she made the occasional exception for chicken wings. As for Wheels, Jack had grown to like him, despite his explosive temperament and tendency to be argumentative for the sake of an argument. He was bat shit nuts for certain. Jack guessed bipolar to be a proper diagnosis for Wheels, but he was most certainly brilliant. Perhaps it was his intelligence that drove him nuts; the sheer frustration of clearly seeing what others could not even comprehend. Jack loved talking to Wheels and listening to his, what appeared to be, wild conspiracy theories on the surface. But after a few hours of mulling the evidence he presented, not really that wild. For sure Jack in his previous life had seen some unbelievable conspiracies come to fruition. Others misjudged Wheels but in a fisticuffs, Jack would choose Wheels over anyone in the ward. He was strong, tactical, and fearless. As far as Dakota, Jack feared for her life. She was young, cute, naïve, and defenseless. It was almost like she had 'victim' tattooed across her freckled forehead. He kept her close. Not that he could defend her, but his Bin gang could.

The tables in the cafeteria sat six. Ward four came in and Gaia sat at Jack's table. She threw her tray on the table, splashing slop onto Dakota. China looked up as Dakota wiped the mess off her pale face. "Apologize, little lady," China said with an open mouthful of black beans, a Bin staple.

Gaia said nothing and started shoveling food into her mouth. Gaia's palate, much like her vagina, was also less than discerning.

"Your white trash mama learn you any manners?" China growled at Gaia.

Gaia banged her fist on the table and methodically stripped off all her clothes and jumped on top of the table. An uninspiring tattoo inquiring "Got Milk?" surrounded her left areola. Her right areola asked, "Got Vodka?". Given the demographics of the Bin, the right nipple was exceedingly in more demand, although the nuance of the "?" may have been overlooked in favor of wishful thinking or risk/reward considerations. Gaia squatted down in front of China and scooped the beans from her plate, smearing the unsavory nutrient all over her face. She commenced screaming like a caged, feral animal: "Get me out of this shithole, you damn Nazis!" She rhythmically danced around the table like a wiccan on bath salts and acid, repeating the chant, and daring anyone to stop her.

"Calm down, little missy, and get off my table." China was staying remarkably calm given the pilfering of her edible sacraments. Jack sat tensed, waiting for China's notorious hair-trigger switch to flip, dreading the certain and violent consequence, yet unable to turn away for what was certain to be the train wreck to follow.

"Lick my hairy cooter, bitch." Gaia's go to insult or, perhaps, legitimate request. One could not be certain. The truth of the phrase lay in the subtleties of its delivery tone and context.

Jack flinched, absent-mindedly protecting his manhood. Surely that was it. Remarkably it was not. China's new meds were impressive. Maybe there was something to modern medicine, Jack thought as he snuck a guilty glimpse. It was indeed a hairy cooter straight from a VW camper in the '70's headed to Woodstock. Inexplicably, he thought back to his days in junior high, a beaver could indeed make a nest in there. In an age of hardwood floors and the occasional nutsack, Gaia had chosen a luscious yet unkept, full shag carpet intended for a 10 x 40-foot 1970's trailer with a disco ball chandler in the abbreviated living area.

"Little lady, you just buying more time in this hellhole," China reasoned. "I been institutionalized 32 times. Wait a minute...31 times." Accuracy in China's institutionalization records was important to the conversation. You never know when you might get fact-checked. That was how Trump lived his life, at least. Never exaggerate. Hyperbole is still a lie. "You got to listen to me. Shut up, get off the damn table, put your britches back on, put away them little pale ass titties, and sit down." China smiled and offered her a hand.

It was like China was a different person; calm and rational in the face of adversity. Jack was impressed to see her de-escalating skills at work. She might have a career as a diplomat, Jack thought. Then the switch got flicked. Gaia kicked China's sacred food tray onto the floor. The change in China was instant, audible, and visible from the international space station. "Houston, we have a problem."

Wheels laughed maniacally. "Dinner and a show."

Dakota shuttered and retreated to the aide's table. The aides watched from a safe distance. Jack stood back, his mouth agape, frozen in anticipation and fear. A creepy smile crossed China's face. "White girl. I ain't changed my period panties in two days and I am gonna stuff 'em down your throat 'til you choke on 'em." China was a woman of integrity. She stripped her pants and panties off, and ungainly climbed onto the table. Jack averted his eyes. Wheel's hurled. The table was no match for the two women's combined weight and collapsed, pinning the two naked women in what resembled a table taco with quad antennas. Gaia continued to yell creative obscenities. China successfully maneuvered and shoved the panties halfway down Gaia's throat as promised, quieting her. China yelled from within the crevice of the table. "You bitches welcome. Now come get me out of here and get me a new plate of food and some new drawers."

A couple of male nurses subdued Gaia, and sedated, covered, and dragged her from the cafeteria. Dakota got China a new plate. An aide brought China a single, paper gown. The group moved to a table where only one person was sitting. Just when Jack thought the show was over for the day, the second act was about to commence. Jack said "hi" to the new guy at their table. China, waiting on a second paper gown to cover her backside, whispered to Jack. "Don't make eye contact." Jack assumed she meant with the new tablemate. The new tablemate reminded Jack of Buckwheat with his braided hair extending from his head in a chaotic manner. He smartly thought better of sharing that observation.

Along with his quirky hair, the new tablemate had crazy crystal blue eyes the color of the Caribbean Sea. He constantly mumbled to himself. All in all he had somewhat of an ethereal yet falling from grace appearance. It was no wonder he was dining alone. He pushed his plate over to China and mumbled. "You want some of my food, fat bitch?"

China did not respond nor make eye contact. This was strange. China did not refuse offered food. Next, he pushed his plate over to Jack. "You want some of my food?" Following China's expert advice on crazy, Jack looked down. "No, thank you," he replied quietly. China kicked Jack under the table.

"Why the fuck I share my food with you, cracker? This here my food. You think 'cause you be white, you entitled to my food."

China looked at me. "Yeah, cracker. I gonna kick your cracker ass when I get you back to the ward. Get your ass up so I can tear it up." She yanked Jack up roughly by his shirt.

Wheels laughed at the absurdity.

China slapped the back of Wheels' head. "Just 'cause you crippled don't mean I won't whip your skinny ass, boy. What, you fall off a tricycle when you an itty-bitty child or you come out your mama pussy like that?" China shook her head. "Roll, Wheels." The crazy man threw his plate at Wheels. Wheels started to respond but China grabbed him and whispered. "Can't win a fight with crazy. That boy got a shiv and don't give a fuck about no consequences."

Dakota pushed her chair back quietly. "And how 'bout you suck my cock, ginger tranny." The ethereal tablemate more demanded than asked.

There was that switch again. The chairs on the ward were too heavy to use as a weapon but here, where all the wards mingled, they unfortunately were not. Bin logic. Safety theater. China slammed the chair into the man's head repeatedly, even after he was motionless. Jack tried to intervene but was not successful, finding himself face down with a nosebleed in pile of black beans. The staff, as per was usual, made no effort to intervene. Finally, Wheels brought China down with a blow to her knees with his chair before she killed the crazy man. China, her blood hot, jumped up to attack Wheels with the agility of a cat tossed in a bath. Jack bear-hugged her trying to calm her. She shook Jack off like a drunk, white coed on a mechanical bull during spring break in Panama City Beach. "Fucking Bin make a sane woman crazy." China looked down at the half-dead crazy man. "Thou art weighed in the balance and found wanting. Ass wipe."

"What the hell, China...The writing on the wall?" Jack asked, wiping blood and beans from his face.

"I know my verses, cracker."

China pulled the sleeve of her gown up to show a faint tattoo. "I will carry out great vengeance on them and punish them in my wrath. Then they will know I am the Lord, when I take vengeance on them." Ezekiel 25:17.

"Jesus," Wheels exclaimed.

"Damn, boy. You crippled and blind. Say right there...'the Lord.'"

CHAPTER TWENTY-FIVE
Outlaw Business

Apache intercepted One Eye as he pulled into the circular drive at the safe house. "We need to go for a ride." One Eye nodded. The two headed south on Beach to a small park a few miles down the road. There, Apache filled One Eye in on the FBI surveillance house next door.

"That's some bullshit." Even One Eye saw through the ruse. "Regardless, we will need to be careful in the house. Let's get half of it cut and packaged and on the street tonight," One Eye explained to Apache. "Already pissed away a day of sales." The two headed back to the house.

Back at the house, Badger grabbed the product and weighed the bag. The bag was five kilos light. "Son of a bitch!" Badger poured the contents onto the counter. Thousands of dead maggots were among the packages.

"That shit's rank," Badger exclaimed just as One Eye and Apache returned.

One Eye observed the contents on the counter without visible emotion. Scribbling on a note pad, Badger wrote, "five kilos short counting the maggots". He continued writing, "...any maggots inside the package, mash into the mix...it'll add some protein to their diet. This batch, cut 50-percent but don't use our branded packaging. Heading out to call Bank".

One Eye returned to the park. "Bad news, Bank. Five short and, what we do have, is infested with dead maggots."

"Do not let trifles vex and distract," Bank replied.

"What the fuck, Bank?"

"Churchill...never mind. Product of an overpriced education. Get it cut and on the street. Fuck the maggots, just grind them in there. They are organic and no worse than any of that other shit we use to cut the product. But don't use our branded packaging."

"Ahead of you on that, Bank."

"Good thinking. Take half the shit to the boys in the campground. Let them start working the bars and campgrounds out on Highway One. You guys start with the strip clubs then head out to the bars on Highway 1 if sales are slow. Stay off Main Street for now. We got a lead on the other half. Any news on the neighbors?"

"Couldn't be more obvious. Looks like a drag queen clown show at a traveling tent revival."

"A show, yeah, but still live and could bite us in the ass. Keep your eyes and ears open. The real threat is coming from another direction. Get back and get that shit on the street."

Half the product was cut and almost packaged by the time One Eye returned. He drank a beer, took a piss, and the Gang was off to the Gold Club in Daytona

Beach. The owner had graciously reserved a VIP area for them and showered them with girls and drinks in exchange for intact limbs and bar security. It was a deal that worked for everyone.

Technically, the Gold Club was a topless club, but this was Bike Week. The owner brought in the traveling A-team and the local police were busy keeping people alive. As such, bottoms found their way to the beer-soaked floor. Other, more carnal, activities were practiced in the seclusion of private rooms out of respect for the family values of the patrons.

One Eye curiously complained. "I hate a bare pussy. When did this hairless fad even start? I mean, what grown ass woman one day woke the fuck up and said 'hey, I want my vagina to look like a ten-year-old's?' And how did she convince the other 3 billion women in the world to think that's a damn fine idea. Let me shave the most sensitive part of my body every other day so I can look like a toddler if per chance some dude sneaks a peek. I feel like a pedo looking at a hairless vagina."

"Damn, One Eye. How do you really feel? That nickel in Starke kinda fucked you up, brother," Apache said.

One Eye replied with a curt elbow to Apache's nose.

Business was brisk. Within a couple hours, the Outlaws were almost sold out. One Eye left Apache and Badger with the remaining product and took the rest of the gang back to the safe house to finish cutting and packaging the product.

CHAPTER TWENTY-SIX
Jack's Genesis Story Part I

25 years earlier.

Somewhat peculiarly, on the cusp of Florence's Old Town, there sits an Irish Pub called the Lion's Fountain. It was a brisk November afternoon and Jack, being Irish, sat on the Pub's patio, downing his fifth, maybe fourth, Guinness while watching the mostly Asian tourists scurry by in the small, Renaissance era square. He found the paradoxes both amusing and bewildering. Jack had fancied a life full of adventure and meaning but his dad insisted he be practical and follow his footsteps into the exhilarating world of accounting. Nothing excites the senses like credits, debits, and journal entries. After a practical and inexpensive multi-directional state school master's in accounting, where Jack's predilection for drinking and debauchery earned him a solid 2.8 GPA, he secured a low-level job with a big pharma company. Seems there was a God.

Shortly, Jack worked his way up to senior analyst, but inexplicably he displayed an unfortunate character flaw that proved worrisome for big pharma…integrity. Conversely, Jack's drinking and debauchery were considered networking and, as such, highly valued assets. However, refusing to "modify" reports to fit the C-suite narrative was a decided and unacceptable liability. Jack was quietly sacked with an amenable going away present and a bulletproof, nondisclosure agreement. The trend continued. This was Jack's third sacking in almost as many years and, thanks to the generous serial severances from the medical community, Jack was both blacklisted and set financially for life short of his 35th birthday. After the last dismissal, he opted for a walk about prior to determining his subsequent career move. Florence was nice in the winter he was told by his then live-in girlfriend. "Pack light," she helpfully advised after grasping this was a solo walk about.

Enter Mary. Slightly older than Jack, she was a tall, beautiful brunette who moved with the confidence, grace, and the menace of a lioness. She spotted Jack on the patio and sat without asking.

Jack's Italian was limited to grazie, buona sera, buon giorno, pizza, prego, spaghetti, and Mario Andretti. Jack typically defaulted to Spanglish whenever speaking to any non-native English speaker, regardless of nationality. Some thought the habit charming, although the younger, over-educated generation tended to see it cringe-worthy at best and often accused Jack of genocide, rape, and pillaging of all native cultures. Jack and Christopher Columbus held much in common. All historical heroes it seems held irredeemable faults, unlike the current generation of keyboard heroes risking cancellation or contrarian responses.

Jack was a bit buzzed and completely dumbfounded by Mary. Fortunately, she spoke first.

"How are you?" Mary asked.

Jack mumbled. "Bien. Y tu?"

The waiter came by. Mary order two espressos.

"You take a wrong turn in Paris? That's easy enough to do, given the lack of signage at de Gaulle airport. But this is Italy, not Spain. Kind of dangerous getting drunk, don't you think? Just how many have you had?"

Jack squinted at her. "Mom, is that you?"

"Cut the shit. We have business to do."

The espresso came. Jack slurped his down and ordered another "cerveza". Mary waved off the waiter after ordering Jack a second espresso.

"Business?" Jack was puzzled. He looked Mary up and down. She didn't look like a hooker and he sure as hell had not solicited one. "Look lady, if my former boss sent you to spy on me, I have not said shit to anyone. I plan to go quietly into the good night. And if you are a working girl, no offense, but I can get ass for free." Jack downed his second espresso and ordered another "cerveza". Mary again waved off the beer for an espresso. Jack would soon be a wide awake and confused drunk.

"As I said, you are in Italy. The word you are looking for is 'birra'."

"That's why they keep bringing me coffee?"

"Look Dougal, cut the bullshit. I flew all the way in from Atlanta to meet with you here. And I find you drunk. You want to pay me $5,000 an hour to play silly games, I'm good. I still get my fee."

"It's Jack and I don't know who you trying to bullshit lady, but they ain't no sane man paying you $5,000 for that ass."

"First off, you misogynist pig, it's my brain they pay me for, not my ass. And your name is what?"

"My name lady...is Jack."

"You are not Dougal from Ireland?"

"Nope. I am Jack from South Georgia. Sorry to disappoint, but I am Irish, if that gets me points."

"Son of a bitch." Mary got up.

"Ouch."

"Not you...well yes, as a matter of fact, you, too." Mary stood angrily. She walked toward the edge of the patio, her heels tapping out her frustration on the wooden deck while dialing her cell.

Jack tried to order another beer, but the waiter told him in broken English the pretty lady had given him $50 Euros not to bring Jack anymore "cervaza".

"That bitch. I knew it. Cervaza is the Italian word for beer."

The waiter scoffed and walked away mumbling about Americans.

Mary walked back over to Jack's table, avoiding every crack in the deck with her stiletto heels without glancing down. Jack pondered the technique. Mary sat as Jack murmured, "magic".

"So I have been told," Mary replied. "My client can't make it and looks as if I have some free time. Let me buy you dinner for disturbing your afternoon pity party."

"What makes you think I'll have dinner with you? You just called me an SOB."

"Please." Mary posed with a hand on her hip, lips slightly parted, eyes fluttering. "Magic."

"Okay. You got a point, but what makes you think this is a pity party? It's a walk about."

"Whatever you need to tell yourself, Jack."

Mary grabbed Jack's arm, wedged a hundred euro under the coffee cup for the tab and walked out of the bar.

"Excuse my French…"

"First, I would need to excuse your Italian."

"Touché…but who the hell are you?"

"Just where are my manners…Mary," she said in a mock Southern accent and extended a gloved hand, "…Attorney at law." She guided Jack to Sasso Di Dante, a quaint cafe just off Duomo Square with a magnificent view of the eternally unfinished Renaissance era cathedral. The café's name roughly translated into Dante's stone. Legend has it Dante watched the cathedral being built from a stone nearby. Likely, the story is Florence's version of "Washington slept here". Mary spoke to the hostess in, what Jack interpreted as, perfect Italian, ordering a bottle of Chianti Classico and the main course for both her and Jack.

"You are a pretty presumptuous broad, aren't you?" Jack meekly protested. The menus were in Italian.

"I could pretend to be offended but I am used to Neanderthals. Comes with the territory, Jack from South Georgia. I represent bad guys. Not assholes like you, not white-collared bad guys, bad guys. Today it was supposed to be an IRA bomb maker."

Jack squirmed in his chair.

Mary laughed. "Don't worry. I was meeting his son. He is 70 and long since retired. I represent Mafia bosses, drug lords, human traffickers, all the worst society has to offer. My biggest client, though, is a motorcycle club. Perhaps you've heard of them. The Outlaws. With those guys, you have to take charge, or the scene can get ugly early."

"Club. Don't you mean gang?"

"Careful, Jack. Those are my clients. Gang implies a criminal enterprise, Jack. Words are like grenades."

"How do you sleep at night?"

"Wow. First time I heard that one. No wonder you don't have to pay for ass with such original lines. First, Jack, if you must know, I charge a shit ton of money. Then, I give two-thirds of that money to causes fighting or helping those who the alleged bad guys harm. Secondly, good wine, great drugs, and anonymous and frequent sex."

"But they just go back out there and do bad shit again. No guilt?"

"Don't be naïve, Jack. If not them, someone else steps up. If there is demand and profit is high enough, someone will supply that demand. Wanna solve the problem...solve the demand side of the equation. You got a better solution, drunk Jack from South Georgia, before you fall off your high horse?"

"Shit, I can't even keep a job."

"Do you ever get laid? And see, even as we speak I am doing a good deed with that evil money by feeding the homeless. Play your cards right and I might even shelter the homeless for a night."

"You hitting on me?"

"Are you a bit slow, Jack? That's rhetorical. It would appear so. I know five-year-old's with better game than you. Convince me otherwise and tell me about what makes Jack, Jack. Make me want to share my bed with you."

Their entrées came. Jack had no clue as to the nature of his entrée but there was some type of pasta and mussels still in their shells in a soupy, unappetizing mix.

"First off, I'm more of a hamburger and fry man."

"Not surprising and not a great start. Give it a try. The old taste buds just might be surprised."

"Not bad. Needs salt." Jack raised his hand to the waiter.

"I will murder your drunk ass with a butter knife, a napkin, and a spoon. I do hope you have a plan B for tonight."

Jack scoffed but put his hand down, realizing she probably only needed two of the three items on her list to complete the task, the butter knife not being one. "First off, my Plan A is to take my uncultured, gameless ass back to the Four Seasons to my suite tonight and empty the mini fridge of overpriced liquor. And, if I get crazy horny, I'll call the concierge to send up a hooker that won't yank my chain. Secondly, what the hell is wrong with a little salt?"

"But you don't pay for ass."

"I make exceptions."

"Okay. Off to a rough start. Let's start with the basics."

"Like what's my sign?"

"Do I look like I'm in high school?"

"That's a lose, lose question."

"Where do you work, Jack?"

"Kinda in between jobs. Thought we covered that."

"Like I never heard that line, but bums rarely stay at the Four Seasons."

Jack laughed and filled her in on his career problem with integrity and big pharma's problem with its lack thereof and the multitude of severances and NDAs. She finished her plate and started eating from Jack's.

"Very presumptuous. Do you ever get laid…I mean, consensually without paying for the privilege?" Jack asked.

"LMAO Jack," Mary deadpanned. "Were you going to eat the rest?"

"Pshaw! That looks like shit on entry. Don't even want to ponder what it might appear as on exit."

"Charming visual. I assume 'Pshaw' is redneck for no."

"It is Southern vernacular for no. You Northerners are so condescending."

"I'm from Atlanta, Jack."

"Anyone north of Macon is the North for a true Southerner."

"So, let me get this straight. You judged me for getting bad guys off the hook and taking their money." She took another of Jack's uneaten muscles. "Kinda seems similar to what you have done with your career. Take the money and look the other way."

Jack took a sip of wine and thought for moment. "It does appear my house is made of glass."

"At least I shed a touch of self-awareness on your pompous ass. I'm sure you donated most of that severance to help the heroin addicts you created."

"Judge much?" Jack asked.

Mary smiled, took a sip of wine, and dabbed the remainder from her red lips with a linen napkin before speaking. "To use, what I believe you termed 'the Southern vernacular', pot…kettle…black."

"Hmph," was Jack's best retort. The wine had slowed his quick wit and she had a point. Then again, he was arguing with someone who got paid $5,000 an hour to do just that. Which was akin to a drunk, lily-white accountant heckling Dave Chappelle from the front row in Detroit.

"So what's next, Jack? Sling some burgers back home?"

"Dunno. I wouldn't take that option off the table. Never wanted to be an accountant. Always wanted a bit of adventure in my life. Saw myself doing something meaningful and maybe a little dodgy. Certainly not pushing numbers around a spreadsheet. Midnight shift at the burger joint drive thru in the hood might not be meaningful but I am betting on adventurous."

"You any good at that accounting thing?" Mary asked, scooping up the last of Jack's uneaten dinner.

Jack snorted. "Surprisingly so for someone who just barely graduated from a directional state school. It's like I have a magical bullshit meter when it comes to numbers. And I don't know where in the hell I got this moral compass from, either. Put the two together, though, and it spells trouble in the corporate world. Well, at least at big Pharma."

"Who knows, Jack? I meet a lot of interesting people who might see your skills and integrity as assets. Maybe someday I can hook you up. But for now…I have an early flight. Come on, big boy."

Jack eagerly pushed his chair back while quoting Bogart. "I think this is the beginning of a beautiful friendship."

CHAPTER TWENTY-SEVEN
Up Skirt

Purdue covered the seat in the truck with paper towels before escorting Horace to the passenger door. The truck was lifted almost as high as Horace's skirt. Purdue failed to avert his eyes in a timely manner. "I didn't sign up for this shit," he mumbled.

"What shit?" Bank asked.

Purdue jumped. "You nervous?" Bank was running through a number of theories on the FBI's strategies. One of them was they had a mole in his crew. Purdue was a valuable earner of the Outlaws but didn't fit the Outlaw mold. Then again, neither did Bank.

"Nope. Just tired of seeing this shit stain's hairy, sagging balls."

"Then cut them off." Bank handed Purdue his knife.

Horace screamed. Purdue squirmed. "Hard pass. He'll just bleed out and we'll be down the missing product."

"Fair point. One Eye called. Fuck tard here still has five kilos of our shit. Come back with all of it or his balls in hand."

Purdue pulled out of the parking lot in the truck with a sobbing Horace. Bank waited a moment and followed. As they drew close to the meth trailer parks, Purdue lightly back-handed the still sobbing Horace. Perversely, the thought of losing the balls he hadn't used in a decade terrified him. "Horace, pull your shit together. I had rather poke my eyes out than cut your balls off."

After a couple of missteps, Horace identified the correct trailer park and, within moments, the precise trailer. Purdue spotted his tail and accurately assumed it was Bank. He grabbed a flashlight from the glove compartment and strolled back to where Bank had parked his bike. "Wanna come help, asshole, or you just wanna play James Bond? You know, a lesser man might think you don't trust him."

"Good thing you're not a lesser man, then, Purdue. Just covering your six." Bank pointed at the truck. "Your boy is running." They both laughed. Horace took three steps and face planted. His feet were bloody from stepping on broken beer bottles. His skirt was up above his ass.

"Damn, Purdue. I owe you an apology. Now, Horace, that's gonna cost you your dick, as well. Better hope the shit is still there. Fetch, boy."

"It's under yonder." Horace, still prone, pointed under the trailer.

"Well get crawling, fuck tard. I ain't going in after it."

Purdue and Bank lifted Horace to his feet and dragged him to side of the trailer. The park was once a nice enough park populated with Midwestern working class retirees escaping brutal winters and high tax rates. All the trailers were once skirted, the park had a pool, a "lake" that was also known as a retention pond to all but real estate agents and commission-reliant property appraisers, and manicured lawns until the meth heads gradually took it over. There was a spot the trailer's skirt had been wedged open. Purdue pointed his light into the area and could see, but not reach, a black plastic bag along with a family of annoyed raccoons that welcomed the light with a series of alarming screeches.

"Like I said, Horace, fetch."

Horace objected. Bank retrieved his knife and held it against Horace's nuts, tightly enough to draw blood, overcoming any previous objections Horace had voiced. Horace took the flashlight and crawled through the opening, exposing his bottom to Bank and Purdue.

"Couldn't you find him any britches?"

"Just thank God it's dark."

The raccoons strongly objected to Horace's trespass. Snarling sounds now accompanied the screeching, smartly encouraging Horace's pace of progress. Surprisingly, within moments, the black bag appeared at the opening. Bank grabbed the bag. "Light," Bank demanded.

Foolishly, Horace handed over the light while still under the trailer. Bank peered into the bag to find the packages compromised by maggots but still largely intact. "Grab the nail gun from the truck," Bank instructed Purdue.

Purdue expected he was on thin ice with Bank, but this was a bit much, he thought. "For what? We got our shit. Let's just leave."

"God forgives…"

Purdue reluctantly retrieved the nail gun while Bank trapped the remarkably resilient Horace under the trailer. Bank spared no nails, even going so far as to circle the trailer, reinforcing the skirting to make an escape more difficult. They walked away to the sounds of Horace's pleas and screams punctuated by the screeching of the raccoons. By the time they drove away, the only sounds were from the raccoons.

CHAPTER TWENTY-EIGHT
Free Horace: The Double Cross Scenario

Puck knew Horace hung out in Zombieland. It was just a matter of finding which derelict trailer he was presently passed out in. Both he and Earl suspected Horace knew the whereabouts of the missing heroin and was the key to recovering their bounty. They borrowed an old F-150 from the farmer and made the paradoxically short passage from paradise to hell. After a couple of unsuccessful passes, Earl spotted a doorless trailer with a front yard that displayed signs of considerable and recent vehicular activity. "Stop here," Earl instructed Puck.

Puck pulled into the front debris field, destroying the last remnants of civilization in the form of a pink flamingo. Both walked through the trailer, carefully avoiding feces, vomit, and needles, but found nothing out of sorts for a Zombieland trailer. Movement under the trailer attracted their attention but they assumed it was rodents that preferred residing in the more sanitary section underneath the domicile. As they exited the trailer, Puck noticed the trailer's skirt had recently been heavily reinforced. "That's odd," Puck remarked.

Horace found the energy to moan quietly and tap on the skirt. Earl went for the crowbar in the truck. The rancid odor coming from underneath the trailer was too much for Earl the shit mucker. Puck finished the job and pulled Horace's barely conscious, raccoon-nibbled, body out. The raccoons chattered. Horace shrieked.

"Damn, dude! Rough day?" Earl had already done the math on how Horace had ended up under the trailer. He tossed Horace a bottle of water from a safe distance and called 911. "Heroin gone?"

Horace guzzled the water and nodded. He looked like a Holocaust victim that did not survive.

"All of it?"

Horace nodded again.

"We are screwed," Puck exclaimed.

"Plan B. But first, let's get out of here before the cops show up. Head to Publix," Earl instructed.

"A little early to do your Fourth of July barbecue grocery shopping now."

"Exactly."

Puzzled, Puck scrunched up his forehead. Horace pleaded for them to wait and protect him from the devils under the trailer until the ambulance came. They did not.

Earl calculated the farmer was inexperienced in the heroin trade and they could pass off flour for heroin. Mix in some Molly or PCP with a brick or two in case he tried to sample or test the product. After gathering supplies, the two headed to Earl's shack to prepare the illusion.

The 911 dispatch center called Earl back. "Hello?"

Fortuitously, it was 'Lucille'. "You called and reported you needed an ambulance in Zombieland," Lucille said, noting the need to file for a bonus for her above and beyond work in returning the call.

"Yes."

"Do you still need an ambulance and, if so, do you have a better location?"

"By now, you might want to send a morgue van. All I can tell you is the trailer doesn't have a door and Horace is laying in the yard by the steps."

"Horace?" Lucille typed in location instructions to the ambulance and police. "And you just left him there?"

"Not my circus. Not my clown." Earl hung up the phone.

The packaging process took several hours but looked surprisingly believable to at least the untrained eye. They called the farmer with the good news. He arranged a meet the next morning at his private airstrip.

The two showed up bathed, with backpacks and two trash bags, one each, of molly-laced 'heroin'. The plane was waiting, and the farmer drove up shortly after dawn accompanied by a goon. The two eyeballed each other. "Implement plan C. Run like hell," Puck whispered.

"Just be frosty."

Surprisingly, the farmer was cordial and took the 'heroin'. He handed Earl an envelope with the agreed upon $10,000. "I'm gonna need your social security numbers to 1099 you for that," he joked. Puck scratched his head.

"What's a 1099?"

The farmer laughed. "Just messing with you because I can."

The pilot started one engine as the two boarded followed closely by the goon. The farmer peeked in and threw the 'heroin' inside the cabin before the goon shut the door. "Safe travels. Enjoy the ride...and the view," the farmer added as an afterthought, laughing.

The plane took off into the bright sunrise and banked a hard 180 degrees shortly thereafter.

Puck asked if there was cabin service. "Mid-flight," the goon grunted.

Earl asked a more relevant question, "Ain't the Bahamas east of here? We seem to be flying west."

"The pilot knows a short cut," the goon answered.

Puck nodded, dreaming of the yacht he would buy with his share of the ten large. He imagined the bikini clad women bringing him frozen drinks with umbrellas and all the Mexican food he could eat in the British Bahamas.

The goon stretched his beefy arms above his head. Earl noticed he was carrying. A sinking reality set in.

CHAPTER TWENTY-NINE
Mandatory Bin Fun

Back at the Bin, Steph was conducting another mandatory group session after the donnybrook in the café. Bin management, fretful on losing its certification for its lucrative Baker and Marchman inmates, had fired the facility manager. As such, a new sheriff was installed who was determined to restore order by any means necessary. China was noticeably missing from the third ward group of scalawags and miscreants. She was a force difficult to overlook. Several newbies had joined the ward, replacing discharged inmates, including Jack's roommate. He had been a quiet Mexican lad who slept his sentence away inexplicably sans mealtimes. Most beds had been filled with new faces, with the exception of one recognizable face from ward four.

Jack raised his hand before Stephanie began. "Where's China?"

"We don't discuss other patients," Stephanie drolly replied.

Jack anticipated a smart-ass response from Wheels. There was none forthcoming. On even a cursory inspection, Jack could tell Wheels was heavily medicated. The mental health modern day version of the lobotomy. Less invasive, but just as effective. Dakota answered Jack. "The goons moved China to ward four." China had been Dakota's roomie.

Stephanie shot Dakota a dirty look. "I would like to speak to you after group," Stephanie growled. Clearly a new mandate had been sent out to the staff to instruct the inmates they no longer ran the prison.

Dakota was finding her voice. "And I you, Spanks."

There was an ever-growing pool of drool under Wheels, threatening a visit from Jim Cantore. "Gale force waves in Central Florida," Jack imagined Jim broadcasting while gripping his helmet as an offscreen intern threw buckets of water at it while simultaneously operating an industrial-sized floor fan for effect. Wheels' head was flopped over onto the armrest. "What the hell did you people do to Wheels? He is fucking catatonic," Jack said, angrily.

"Language, Jack. And that is a symptom of his cerebral palsy."

"First off, bullshit. Secondly, thought you couldn't discuss other patient's medical information, Steph." Jack was channeling Wheels. His level of patience and compliance to the institution's rules had worn thinner than his hair with the passage of time.

Steph ignored Jack's comments and continued railing about the inappropriate behavior of the patients as if it wasn't the failure of the institution's policies that had caused the melee to begin with. She outlined the consequences of said ill-advised behavior, including restricting outdoor time (there was virtually none… half-hour on days the staff deemed were nice enough), restricting television time (it was barely watchable with only channels U and 3 broadcasting born-again sermons and required an inmate to hold the rabbit ears in place between a precise 83- and 84-degree angle), and eliminating snacks "beginning immediately". It was at this point Stephanie realized exiting the room for safety purposes served her best interest. Given the horrific food, lack of entertainment (aside from a few ironically left behind Dorsey serial murder novels), boorish and dehumanizing treatment by the staff, snack time was one of the few moments of joy for the inmates. Steph had crossed the Rubicon, touched the third rail, woke the bear.

Dakota snagged Jack's arm and followed Stephanie into her office. "Jack, you can leave. This is a private, patient-doctor conversation."

"Stephanie, if you're a doctor, I'm the pope. Check that, the second coming of Jesus Christ, and I damn you and this entire staff to the seventh ring of eternal hell. Wanna stick with doctor? I got my damning tool at the ready." Jack grabbed his crotch. Several exes on his departure had assured him it was not worth a damn. Jack strongly disagreed with the majority.

"Like I said, inappropriate behavior will now be met with immediate consequences. You will stay in your room and miss lunch today, Jack."

Jack laughed uncontrollably. "Don't threaten me with a good time, Mom. Have you ever eaten that shit? Makes me miss public high school cafeteria food."

Dakota spoke up. "I would like to change roommates." She had landed the ward four transfer.

"We don't allow patients to choose roommates, Dakota."

"She is making sexual innuendos and I'm scared of her. Jack doesn't have a roommate. Can I room with him?"

"We can't allow two people of the opposite sex to room together."

Dakota rolled her eyes. "Eww. First off, Jack is a fat ass and is old enough to be my granddad."

"Ouch! I can hardly wait to hear second off," Jack mumbled.

"Second, you do know I am transgender, right?"

"But you identify as female. We have to respect that."

Jack spoke up. "Can I go on the record for a moment? I just now figured it out. I, too, identify as a woman. Apparently a fat, old, ugly one like you. That fix it for you, Steph? And by the way, I can see your spanks. Represent, sister." Jack raised his hand to high five her. She left him hanging. Dakota giggled. Jack remembered covid safety protocols before he was an inmate and moved to a fist bump. He was still left hanging.

Steph struggled to cross her legs. "Still, can't have patients selecting roommates."

"Okay…I'll give you a moment to do some mental math. You have a ward four patient who outweighs Dakota by 50…60 pounds in her room. Dakota has notified you in front of a witness, albeit judged mentally unstable…and fat…" Jack gave Dakota a dirty look. He continued. "She is frightened of her. I don't know why her roomie was on ward four but guessing not because she is a saint. Should Dakota get raped or beaten or both, it's on you, baby girl. Feel me? If you can't put her in with me, put her in with one of those old, drunk ladies. But get her the hell out of that room. And I tell you what, I'll happily keep skipping meals and pills until you do." Jack thought reminding Steph of the problems of rapes and murders that had previously occurred at the Bin and been reported in the local news might draw some attention. It did.

Shortly after, two burly men showed up at Jack's door, armed with tasers and night sticks. Seems the new sheriff hired deputies. They roughly escorted Jack to the detox room, the mental hospital's version of solitary. It was there Jack heard the sweet roar of motorcycles. "I love you, Mary," Jack mumbled.

∞∞∞∞

Bank protested. "Jesus, Ax. We just got back to Daytona with the rest of the merch."

"Not my call, brother. Leave a couple guys at the house to finish up but take the rest back to Ocala, toot sweet, and spring Jack from that loony bin you already shot up. Here is a bonus for you…that Jack fellow owns the FBI surveillance house next door, and he did not give them permission to use it. And, by the way, Jack… he's Mary's husband."

"Mary, Counselor Mary? Who the hell knew she was married?"

"Complicated story, apparently. But Mary has juice," Ax unnecessarily noted.

Bank replied. "I get it, but two guys here can't perform suitable security on the house and get the product ready to sell."

"We both know that security house is a ruse. FBI has another angle. That's what you need to be worried about."

"Yeah…thinking a rat," Bank said.

"All seems like a lot a work for a drug bust," Ax pondered out loud. A couple years prior, the FBI had raided two of the Outlaws' Daytona area houses and came up with diddly squat except for a couple of Outlaw jackets as parting gifts. "Maybe payback? Beats me. The agents are going by the code names of Barnes and Noble. Apparently operating on the rouge side is their MO."

"Yeah, we ran into the clowns a couple times. Gucci gangster as shit. They shot up the loony bin, for the record. We just followed them in."

"I'll send a couple of brothers from the campground to provide security for the safe house. Ride the Indian with the tracking device to Ocala. Maybe that will pull the dickheads away, as well."

"What we do with Jack once when we get him?"

"Bring him home and watch the fireworks. Mary is coming to town to meet him to paper those FBI fools."

"Damn, I love that woman."

"We all do, Bank. Now go get her husband out of the Bin."

∞∞∞∞∞

Apache appropriated a garbage truck, which he promptly procured and drove through the plywood covered front doors of the Bin. Subtlety was not his strong point. The receptionist ducked under her desk, hovering above a puddle of fresh pee. The blanket previously on her lap soaked the floor pee up. Apache blasted the horn and stuck his head out the window. "Here's Johnny," he yelled, maniacally. The receptionist froze. Apache, Outlaw or not, didn't have the heart to run her over. "Ma'am, you might want to move your fat ass. I'm playing through." He revved the engine to its limits. The receptionist attempted to run but was pulled down by the wet blanket wrapped around her cankles. She crawled on all fours, creating a wet path of hand and knee prints to a location five yards away. She yanked the piss-soaked blanket over her head in an attempt to protect herself with the only available item. "Suit yourself," Apache muttered. He blasted through the inner doors and backed out of the massive hole he had created. Seven Outlaws poured through on Harleys and one on an Indian.

Sirens quickly followed. Apache backed over two police vehicles before getting stuck on a third, where he dumped his rancid load mostly for self-satisfaction, but never-the-less proved an effective distraction. Apache hustled into the building. The police called for the SWAT team from Orlando for assistance only to be informed they were occupied in a shootout with armed 11- and 13-year-old male and female suspects who had escaped from a juvenile facility and taken a McDonalds' staff and diners hostage with a pair of plastic sporks. Purdue located the new Bin administrator surrounded by his new hired muscle. "How we gonna play this, Chief?" Purdue asked. "The easy or hard way?"

The administrator was a tough guy. He was an ex-prison warden from Starke. The transition to a mental health facility in Ocala, Florida made perfect sense in the world of for profit health care. Pretty much the same mission. He had dealt with plenty of Outlaws before, but not without being surrounded by armed guards and locked cages. "As I see it, there are three of us and one of you. I suggest you lie face-down on the ground and beg for mercy, asshole," the administrator brazenly responded.

"Excellent math skills, Big Boss Man. Let me suggest an alternative solution. I'm just here for a patient of yours being held against his will. Fellow named Jack Smith. Old guy tried to off himself I hear. No danger to

society. Hand him over and we are out of your hair...
metaphorically speaking."

"Get 'em, boys," the administrator ordered.

Purdue was a salesperson by trade. He held up his
finger. "Let's put a pin in that, fellows. What is this bald,
fat asshole paying you? Maybe $35,000 a year? Now
me, yeah, you can kick my ass but you gotta figure,
I'm likely not here by myself. Risk...reward. Don't you
need to go take a piss or something?"

Purdue thought his speech convincing. Unbeknownst
to him, Apache, Bank and One Eye had come up silently
beside him. The guards suddenly found an urgent need
to empty their bladders. Meanwhile, the rest of the
Outlaws had rounded up the staff and placed them all
tightly in the confines of the nurse's station.

"Seems the formula has evolved. Face down on
the floor, Big Boss Man." One Eye added convincing
touches until Big Boss Man complied. Bank placed his
knee on the administrator's neck. "Where is Jack, tough
guy?"

"Detox," he mumbled.

"Keys."

"Top desk drawer."

One Eye rifled through the drawer. "Hustler, lotion,
Asian teens, lady boys, keys. You ever heard of the
internet?" One Eye kicked Big Boss Man in the temple
with his steel toe boots, dropping the porn magazines
on his lifeless body.

"Was that necessary?" Purdue asked.

"I'm having a bad day. That traffic was brutal from
Ormond. Fucking biker wanna-be's with their New
York tags can't ride for shit."

"Yet still, seems a bit of an overreaction," Purdue
replied.

One Eye stepped to Purdue. "You don't get it 'cause you will never really be one of us. The bald fellow on the ground. He was the warden at Starke. I gave him a swift death. He's lucky I don't have more play time."

The nurses directed Purdue to the detox room. "A bit of an upgrade from Starke," One Eye noted.

"You Jack?" Purdue asked.

"Who's asking?"

"Mary sent us. Let's ride, old man."

"A couple favors first."

"You're shitting me, right? Not holding any leverage to ask for favors, old man," One Eye replied.

Jack responded. "Not shitting you, man. Package deal. I'm not leaving without Wheels, Dakota, China, and a little payback."

Bank had joined them and pointed toward the door. "There's cops outside. Kinda need to blow this nut house."

"Don't change shit. Not leaving without them. Explain that to Mary."

Bank shook his head in surrender correctly calculating breaking patients out of a nut house was easier than going round for round in an argument of logic with Mary. "Where the hell do I find these circus freaks of yours?"

"Dakota is a little redhead on ward three. Just need someone to take her to meet up with her mom and get her out of this hellhole. China is a very large African-American woman on ward four. You'll like it there." Jack pointed to ward four.

"You know Outlaws don't normally do black," One Eye said.

"Not asking you to do her, just get her the hell out of here. Be careful, she might kick your ass, though. She is a bit cuckoo for cocoa puffs." Jack circled his fingers arounds his ears in the universal sign of crazy.

"Ain't no woman gonna kick my ass," One Eye boasted.

"Tell yourself whatever will help you sleep at night, brother."

"You ain't my brother," One Eye noted.

"Damn, did we wake up on the wrong side of the bed?"

One Eye charged at Jack. Bank grabbed him. "His blood is up. I would go easy on him, Jack." Bank turned to One Eye. "Hey, asshole...Mary's husband. Stay focused. We are on the clock. Go gather up this China broad."

"Where do we find this Wheels?" Bank asked.

"Easy peasy. He'll be in his room down this hall." Jack pointed down the corridor. "It's room 2B. He has cerebral palsy. He's not a nice man, but one you might want to consider adding to your tribe."

"Tribe? Do we look like Indians or Jews?"

"Damn, everybody's so sensitive. But to be frank, you don't look much like cowboys, either. So...gang, fraternity, club, cult...what the hell ever. Wheels is brilliant, like frigging Einstein smart. He's lacking any moral compass and he's freakishly strong. Just got to get over the asshole part, wild mood swings, slurring speech, inability to walk, gambling, drinking, whore-mongering, and he will fit right in."

"Did I ask for the dweebs whole fucking life story? Tick tock, asshole."

"2B," Jack pointed down the hall. "Just trying to do your fraternity a solid."

Bank shot Jack a bird as he went off in search of Wheels. Jack found the nurse who had stripped searched him and left him without any clothes but an ill-fitting hospital gown and no drawers for over a day. "Go grab me some hospital gowns, darling. It's time to party." He instructed everyone to strip buck-naked. At first they resisted. Apache hammered on the counter. The disrobing process sped up exponentially. Steph stepped out of her spanks to an explosion of pent-up flesh that reverberated down the halls, illustrating the Doppler effect.

There were about 25 employees crammed into a small area, each trying to cover their privates as best they could while covertly checking out their neighbors' parts. "How does it feel to be dehumanized?" Jack asked. "This is what you do to everyone. People with real mental problems who walk through your doors. Now, bend over and touch the floor and cough. Feels nice, right? Sets you on the path to recovery. That feeling, I imagine, is gonna stay with you for a while. Might even send you to therapy. Now, throw me your clothes."

Jack tossed the clothes on the floor and began pissing on them. "Yes, that's piss. Try to stay warm," Jack said, never breaking eye contact with his initial torturer. "Don't look away, it's not like you hadn't already seen my dick, darling." Apache joined in laughing maniacally. Jack threw them hospital gowns. "You can cover up with these now. Fortunately for you, this will only last a couple hours. Imagine a couple days. Maybe you learned something today, but probably not. If you can be nothing else in here, for God's sake, be kind. Kindness is both priceless and free. Fucked-up people walk through these doors. They're at their most vulnerable. Most of you assholes treat them as non-humans. When you go home tonight and suckle your baby, kiss your partner, play with your dogs, and lay your pretty little heads on your pillow, I want you to take a minute and face the evil in what you do. You are not unlike the Germans in the towns adjacent to concentration camps who ignored the atrocities under their noses and profited on the slaughter of innocents. I hope this provides a taste of what that feels like. Society is judged by how they treat their most vulnerable members."

Bank looked at Jack. "Hyperbole much? You just might belong in this place, dude."

"No argument. Rough day. You go a couple weeks without a drink, decent meal, private shit, and you get a little irritated, hangry…and thirsty."

"Point taken."

One Eye located China. She was hard to miss. China had seized the opportunity to break into the snack closet and was currently encircled by empty snack packaging. "You China?" One Eye asked brusquely.

"Yeah, cracker. What you want? You see I'm busy here."

"Jack sent me to get you."

"Well, Jack can jack off. I ain't going nowhere with the likes of you. I'm on vacation. This is my Club Med, and I ain't interrupting it with a KKK excursion to a church burning with your ugly ass. You got seven young 'uns, cracker?"

"Fuck if I know." One Eye was a bit taken aback.

"Well, how many women you raped, cracker? That'll seriously narrow down the possibilities. Can't imagine many give it up to your ugly ass willingly."

"The state accused me of three…but I only did time for one," One Eye replied incongruously with pride.

"Well, look at you. Ain't you one pitiful mother fucker."

"You the fat bitch in the loony bin, stuffing her face with cookies and candy."

China stuffed an entire Mars bar into her face. "In here, cracker, I sleep, eat, and watch tv and somebody even clean my room once a month for free. Out there, my young'uns, mama, grandma, my aunties, all bug the shit out of me to work and clean. You get your ass on up out of here 'fore I whip it for that smart mouth and that Nazi tattoo on your neck. Yeah, I see it, you racist mother fucker."

The chaos of the day was too much for Gaia. She stripped naked and ran through the ward, passing China and One Eye while screaming her usual rants of, "Eat my hairy cooter", and "Get me the fuck out of here".

One Eye took a long look at Gaia. "God bless America," One Eye lustfully exclaimed.

"Gaia, now that bitch is crazy, fool. I think she might just be your soulmate, cracker."

"When you are in a nut house, aren't you all crazy?" One Eye asked.

"When you in a prison, ain't you all criminals? Crazy's relative, cracker." China called out to Gaia. "Gaia, get that hairy cooter over here."

Gaia sauntered over to China ready to do battle. One Eye's eyes grew larger with each step.

"This here cracker...what your name, fool?" China asked.

"One Eye," he replied as he uncharacteristically reached out to kiss Gaia's hand like she was naked Guinevere and he, albeit demented and tatted, Sir Lancelot. Gaia cuffed him hard across his unshaven face. One Eye beamed like a five-year-old on Christmas morning and wiped the spittle and a spot of blood from his mouth with his bare, grizzled arm.

"Given the swell in his britches, this here cracker crushing on your nasty ass and want to sweep your skanky ass out of here. Y'all will probably make some retarded Nazi babies and shit."

Gaia cupped One Eye's face and sucked his tongue out of his mouth while gyrating in his lap.

"Damn crackers ain't got a bit of no morals," China exclaimed. "Take that shit on the road 'fore I toss my cookies. Now you two go out there and make America great again!"

Gaia snagged a hospital gown on the way out of the Bin and rode bitch three-quarters naked with One Eye, pressing her breasts tightly against his back. One Eye silently rehearsed his proposal speech, discarding one after another as too sappy until he settled on "Marry me, Bitch". Wheels, still drugged, perilously hung on to Purdue for dear life with the assistance of a bungie cord and a generous amount of duct tape. Jack sat behind Bank. Bank swatted away Jack's hands as he tried to hold on for dear life. The rest of the Outlaws waited near the Bin until they were clear and led the police in the opposite direction.

CHAPTER THIRTY
The FBI Agents Barnes and Noble

Barnes answered his phone from Buckets, a beach dive bar on the cusp of Ormond Beach and Daytona. He was watching a dozen or so half-naked, drunk biker chicks try to play something that loosely resembled volleyball on ice. "This better be something worth my time, asshole. I'm kinda busy." Noble frowned.

"You said let you know if we get hit on the tagged bike moving," the agent said coyly.

"Yeah, so," Barnes replied, annoyed with the interruption.

"Well, we got a hit."

"So, where is the bike heading?" Barnes asked.

The agent hesitated. "Well, sir, I really don't know. It just started moving."

"You're more worthless than an anal douche bag in a lesbian whore house."

Noble indignantly flipped him off. Barnes scoffed and shrugged his shoulders.

"Call me when you know something. The big-breasted, bleached blond just took her top off." Barnes hung up the cell, snapped a photo, and sipped from his umbrella-adorned frozen concoction.

"You know I'm gay, right, asshole? And that shit is offensive as hell. Come to think of it, you are a giant misogynist," Noble replied.

Barnes studied her for a moment. She was attractive. He had never taken stock. She had shoulder-length, light red hair, large green eyes, a lightly freckled and petite nose, and a small but fit body. He took a long draw on his frozen drink. "No shit, Noble! Can I watch?" Barnes asked.

"There are rules now, Barnes. It's not the wild west anymore, even in the macho FBI. You get fired for saying shit like that."

A waitress passed by, and Barnes flagged her down, ordered two shots of tequila and turned back to Noble. "You mean, macho rules like not pistol whipping a 60-year-old man in a nut house or shooting up said nut house? Me, I consider rules to be more like helpful guidelines. You, I guess, are a strict by the book agent? How's that drink, by the way?"

The shots came. Barnes' cell rang. He lifted his glass to toast Noble. Their glasses clinked before they tossed the drinks back. "What the hell now," Barnes answered.

"You said…"

"I know what I said. Spit it out, dumbass."

"The bike is heading west on Highway 40. It just passed I-95…"

Barnes hung up the cell and turned to Noble. "Why would those assholes be going back to Ocala?"

"To collect the rest of their heroin from whoever stole it."

"Nah. The Outlaws retrieved the rest of their product. Makes no sense to return to Ocala. Call your CI," Barnes instructed.

"Too dangerous. Let's get an agent from Orlando to check it out." Noble called the SAC in Orlando. His assistant answered the phone. Noble left an urgent message with a priority code. The assistant promised to pass on the message but said the office was swamped with a high priority mission.

Barnes and Noble continued enjoying the devolving volleyball match as it slowly turned into more of a hard, R-rated orgy while they sipped frozen drinks; every bartenders' nightmare during high season. With Barnes' new knowledge of his partner's sexual proclivities, he somehow felt closer to her as they now perversely had something in common: hot chicks. And, as the drinks flowed, their hate/love bond grew stronger.

Some hours later, the Orlando SAC returned Noble's call. "What you got?"

Noble took a moment to gather her thoughts before answering. "We need a couple agents to surveil a suspect heading to Ocala".

"No can do, agent."

"You didn't let me finish."

"Well, it sounds like you already finished several, and we have every agent available here working overtime on a high priority case. Not even a file clerk here we can cut loose."

"May I ask what foreign head of state was kidnapped in Orlando?"

"Don't be a wise ass with me, Noble. I've read both you and your partner's jackets. Why the hell either of you are still in the FBI is beyond my paygrade."

"Exactly, asshole. Now what is your big case?"

Barnes got a little wood listening to the conversation before remembering Noble's propensity for the fairer sex.

"Disney."

"Disney what? Somebody plant a bomb, gang rape Cinderella, chop Mickey's ears off, or kidnap Pluto?"

"No."

"Then what?"

"Trademark infringement case," the SAC gruffly replied. Disney had juice in Orlando.

"You got to be kidding me." Noble hung up the phone and turned to Barnes. "Let's roll."

"Yeah…" Barnes said, attempting to stand… "I don't think we can do that".

Noble called for an Uber. A half hour later, the Uber showed up, saw the pair, thought better of it, and drove off. She called a second Uber, and, after another half hour, the driver arrived. Before he could flee, Noble offered him an extra $100 for the ride. The driver warned there was a $300 clean up fee for puking. They headed west to Ocala.

Bike traffic was heavy, and the ride was deliberate. Barnes asked the driver to stop for a six pack. The driver declined. Barnes flashed his FBI badge. The driver said his five-year-old had one as well. Noble whispered in Barnes' ear. "We are in the middle of nowhere. Let's not piss this guy off."

Barnes interrupted her as they passed Barberville. "Look, a giant fucking rooster next to the Statue of Liberty." The driver shook his head. Noble shrugged in apology. Barnes' cell phone rang.

"They appear to have stopped at the Pines," the agent from the surveillance house advised.

"The Pines? The nut house...where crazy Jack is?"

"Affirmative."

Barnes hung up the phone. "Turn us around, man."

"With pleasure," the driver responded.

CHAPTER THIRTY-ONE
Jack's Genesis Story Part II

23 years earlier.

Jack was day drinking at the split in Caye Caulker, Belize at the Lazy Lizard with a couple of quirky ex-pats and a few salty locals. Caye Caulker is a tiny, still relatively unspoiled island split in half in the early sixties by a hurricane. The coral island is located on the second longest living barrier reef in the world. It is popular with the almost rich kids; the backpacking crowd spending daddy's retirement or the few bucks of student loan money remaining in their accounts for a gap year...or four. Adulting didn't start 'til thirty, and work was overrated and for the small-minded lacking vision. Divers, fishermen, and expats blended in among the friendly locals, creating a peculiar and engaging gathering. Barney, one of many of the town's colorful expat drunks, handed Jack his phone and another shot of tequila. He had a text from Mary. "Call me from somewhere private." Mary and Jack had kept in touch and occasionally saw each other, but her career kept her too busy for a real relationship. Jack even briefly moved to Atlanta but found himself alone most of the time. He then moved to Belize where he found Barney to be better company and the occasional backpacker with daddy issues to satisfy his other, more carnal, needs.

Jack dialed Mary's number from the bar.

Mary answered. "You're at the Lizard scoping the back sides of coeds."

"Lucky guess. Not like you show me yours. And, for the record, most have already graduated college."

"Still pervy. This is serious. Some guy is going to drop you a burner phone at your shack. Answer the phone when it rings. I can vouch for the person on the other end. Gotta run. Miss you." She hung up the phone.

"What the..."

Barney passed Jack another shot. "Shaken, not stirred." They touched glasses. Barney winked at a coed. She shot him a bird. "Paradise lost," Barney lamented.

And so began Jack's brief career working for a black ops arm of the NSA in Afghanistan. Mary had numerous federal intelligence agents in her virtual rolodex. Sporadically, she came across an agent with integrity. Ironically, Mary was working the IRA bomber case when she met with "Bob", one of those rare agents she trusted implicitly to play the game hard but who was always fair. Over coffee and idle chatter, he mentioned he was searching for someone with integrity, accounting skills, and a pharmaceutical background. Mary smiled. "Bob, I'm disappointed. I thought I knew you better."

Bob blushed. "Am I that easy? Maybe I should change careers. We have a job that we think would be great for Jack."

"I'm not going to even ask how you know Jack and I know each other, but you are buying today and I'm changing all my passwords."

Bob laughed. "Give us a little credit. Jack has been on our radar for quite some time. You don't stack up that many NDAs from big pharma without us taking notice. So, relax with the passwords. We found your connection with Jack by tracking Jack. Have to be straight. It does not come without a bit of danger. It's off the books and in sand land."

In spite of her instincts, she agreed to pass the message on to Jack on one condition; Bob would do everything in his power to extract Jack if he got in over his head. If she had realized she was sending Jack into yet another lion's den, she may have had second thoughts.

∞∞∞∞

A year later....

Jack was on the run. His integrity had once again proven a liability. Half the US government agencies and contractors in the Middle East were tracking him down. He had discovered massive fraud across the region, spilling into India and Africa. He had not found the end of the tentacles. Big pharma was dumping non-FDA approved and expired medicines and charging the governments and NGO's multiples of retail. Naturally, a string of kickbacks kept everyone quiet. The paper trail really was not that hard to uncover. A Chinese third-grader with an attitude and an overbearing grandmother could have found the fraud. An American third-grader would have found a booger, a pencil eraser, and a half-eaten crayon. Yeah, China is gonna kick our ass.

An SVR agent, Yuri, had befriended Jack. Or, quite possibly, as Jack came to realize, had compromised him. Yuri showed Jack evidence of US forces and agencies cooperating with tribal leaders in Afghanistan to include providing arms, cash, intelligence, and troops to combat rival tribes in exchange for assisting with the logistics of moving "legal" drugs and arms throughout the mid-east. It was spookily reminiscent of El Chapo and the disastrous war on drugs in Mexico leading to carnage. The enrichment of the arms industry had been transplanted to the mid-east. Compromised or not, Jack believed the evidence and corruption unassailable.

Yuri confiscated Jack's cell phone and deftly deposited the phone in a morgue wagon drawn by a cantankerous donkey. Yuri secreted Jack out of Kabul to a village at the foot of the mountains in a beater Toyota truck, the favored vehicle of your average global terrorist.

"You guys ever considered driving a Ford?" Jack asked.

"Toyota give terrorist and Russian spook good discount. Good gas mileage. Free satellite radio. Ford stand for Fix Or Repair Daily. Toyota good truck. Take licking, keep ticking." Yuri pulled up in front of a mud hut with several bearded men outside and sitting around an open fire. "Here is where I leave you now. May Allah protect and guide you."

"What the hell, man. I'm an accountant. I count beans in an air-conditioned office for a living. I can't do this spy shit." Jack was rethinking his adventure dream. Maybe his dad was right.

"No, Jack. You spy now. And I'm old. I can't walk through the mountains. That's a stupid man's game."

Yuri laughed. He was old. He had fought for the Soviets in the mid-80's, facing what the Americans then called the Freedom Fighters, and supplied with weapons, training, and intelligence courtesy of the United States taxpayer. Decades later, the same group was called the Taliban and the Russians supplied them with similar tools of the trade. The circle of life. Yuri stayed in the country as KGB, then later the SVR with a friendly tribal leader.

Yuri introduced Jack to his guide, Mohamad, who spoke little English and was not fond of Americans. "This should be fun," Jack murmured.

"You want I can take you back. Let your NSA friends give you a one-way trip in morgue wagon for dirt nap," Yuri offered.

Over the next several grueling weeks, Mohamad grudgingly guided Jack and a small entourage of three armed men through the mountains via Toyota truck, horseback, but mostly on foot, until they entered Pakistan. Conversation was light, limited mostly to grunts, jeers, and angry gestures for Jack to keep up. At the border, Jack was delivered to a second SVR agent without introduction, ceremony, or a proper goodbye to his fellow travelers with which he had developed a deep and everlasting bond that psychiatrists refer to as Stockholm Syndrome. On the positive side, the agent had an air-conditioned vehicle, a bottle of water, and a sandwich of known origin. Once sated, Jack began to worry about the optics of cooperating with so many SVR agents. Then, he considered the optics of being eaten by worms. It was, as they say in the pros, a fifty-fifty ball.

The agent had yet to speak a word to Jack, which was fine by Jack who slept. He awoke after an undetermined passage of time alongside a makeshift dirt airstrip straight out of a Mexican cartel telenovela. A derelict, small, two-engine plane sat on the strip with one prop begrudgingly turning, prepared for departure. A lone gunman stood by the open door. Jack asked the agent to see the plane's maintenance records.

The agent handed him a passport, a ticket to Bangkok, a baseball hat with a rainbow multicolored peace sign, a few thousand rupees, and a backpack. The agent pointed at the plane and spoke. "The plane or that mountain path will take you to Katmandu. As you infidels say, 'dealers choice'. There, someone will meet you and give you further instructions."

"Katmandu. That's a real place?" Jack asked. "Thought it was a Raiders of the Lost Ark fictional location."

"Fucking Americans." The agent reached across Jack, opened his door, and roughly pushed him out.

"I'll miss you, too, buddy." Jack blew him a kiss and crossed himself as he entered the plane.

"Your God and that rainbow hat will get your head separated from your body in this country," the gunman said in perfect English.

"I'll find the first mosque in Katmandu and convert if this rust bucket gets me there alive."

The gunman laughed. "For real, man. You can't do that cross shit in these parts. There are some real hard cores around who will take your head and ask questions of it for several days later."

"Where you from?" Jack asked.

"Michigan."

Jack laughed. "But of course," he muttered to himself and boarded the plane.

The plane safely landed at a private strip in Nepal with accumulated deferred maintenance. A third, likely Russian agent, equally humorless, delivered Jack into the most crowded part of Katmandu's old city he could possibly locate. There was a sea of humans, animals, and every form of transportation known to man from the beginning of time. The agent gave Jack an address for a hotel with instructions to not leave the room.

"I think I am obligated to find a mosque," Jack replied.

The agent pointed a Glock at Jack. "If you want death, this will be less painful."

"Jesus Christ, can anybody take a joke around here?" Several passersby stopped and glared at Jack before moving on. "I think I got my answer."

It took Jack three hours, all of his patience, and most of his cash to find the hotel. "If this is a fucking audition for The Amazing Race, I'm not interested," Jack mumbled to no one in particular. His Nepali was a little rusty, so he defaulted to Spanish. "Donde esta hotel ...", and, as such, the monetary exchange rate flexible for the unintelligible information offered. Fortunately, the Russians thought this through and had included another sandwich and water in Jack's backpack. Certainly, if there was a tail, Jack lost them in his accidental tour of the city's crowded and untoward sites. Eventually, Jack stumbled upon the hotel. It was five and a half stars short of a two-star hotel. The bed manifested an entire eco system without the aid of a blacklight. The doorless, unisex bathroom was down the hall to the left and comprised of a hole in the floor outlined with a dabble of urine, feces, and (probably) menstrual blood...destination unknown. A 55-gallon drum of light brown water besieged with anonymous flotsam was provided for bathing. Jack opted to forgo bathing, and shit in the mop bucket without grasping the requisite physics of the offered appliance for said purpose. Jack, using his backpack as a pillow and his shoe as a weapon, slept on the floor where the creatures were at least large enough to see in the dark and, consequently, unable to crawl inside of any bodily orifices.

The next morning, at first light, an old Nepali woman banged on his door like a drill sergeant waking recalcitrant trainees after their first weekend pass consumed with pent up debauchery. She brought a traditional Nepali breakfast. Jack was dubious of its contents or of his stomach's capacity to retain it and smartly chose not to face the terrors of the communal bathroom again. He drank what appeared to be tea. Shortly after, a burly Russian man gathered him and transported him to the airport in a car the size of a macranganin nut. En route, the Russian handed Jack a coach ticket to Jakarta, a few thousand rupiah, and an address to a hotel.

"You guys too cheap to spring for first class?"

"Fucking Americans. Keep the hat on and maybe take a bath. You smell like camel shit."

No one met Jack at the airport in Jakarta. He found a cab in the chaos that took him to the hotel. Thankfully, it deserved the entirety of the one star it had been awarded. Jacked bathed, found fresh clothes in his closet, grabbed a rice dish from the hotel's café (or perhaps the employee refrigerator), and slept in the bed after discarding the pillow and bedspread. The next morning, no one came for him. Morning turned to night. Jack stayed in the room, fearful to go out and miss his ride to his next exotic destination. He could only assume the indirect route to wherever they were taking him was a security measure, although it felt more like Yuri was just messing with him.

The knock came early evening, and the routine was repeated. Jack was delivered to the airport with a ticket to Bangkok, a handful of Bahts, and an address to a hotel. The hotel was in the heart of Bangkok's red-light district which explained his driver's look of disgust. A popular sex tourist destination, the hotel was agreeable, even if the occupants were sleazeballs. Starving, he went out for dinner and had a couple of beers. He was interrupted by several propositions for innumerable varieties of sex, some unintelligible by the uninitiated, by what he could only assume were Bangkok's famous lady boys. "Inverted donkey kick. What the f... Never mind." Jack politely declined. The next morning, breakfast came and, fortunately, was a typical western breakfast, likely indicating the hotel's dominant clientele. After devouring his breakfast, Jack spent the day in the room and, at both lunch and dinner, room service arrived without having ordered it. He became apprehensive.

The next morning, a lady boy knocked on his door. "No, thank you," Jack said. He went to close the door, only to find a six-inch, red stiletto blocking the door.

"Come with me, Jack. I don't bite. You are not my type," she added, shaking her head in disgust.

Jack wasn't sure if he should be flattered or insulted, but he followed her to a rickshaw waiting in the street. The female agent handed him a ticket to Dili but no cash. "Someone will pick you up at the airport."

"One question, where the hell is Dili?"

"Damn westerners...East Timor."

"Well, that certainly helped. Just to get my bearings, assuming that is just to the east of West Timor?"

"Ditch the stupid hat," the agent, unamused, advised. She shot Jack the universal sign of contempt as she parted his company.

"That went well," Jack mumbled. "I think she is into me."

The plane ride was largely uneventful. The pilot apologized for the AC malfunctioning. His seatmate apologized for her rooster's diarrhea. Jack managed to nap.

Jack exited the plane and made his way through the small terminal without event. There, he found Mary waiting for him on the sidewalk. Jack fell to his knees, unconsolably sobbing. He looked up into her eyes and quoted Bogart. "Of all the gin joints in all the towns, she walks into mine."

Mary drove Jack to a small beach hotel. "Rough few days, buddy? Gotta say, the trip took those few extra pounds you were carrying off. Kinda digging the lean, scruffy Jack look. I'd do you...after a Clorox bath or two."

Jack had gotten ahold of himself. "Disney should add this adventure as a new theme park. Dante's inner circle of hell. Get the shit scared out of your entire family and lose those extra pounds for $200 a day! Plus accommodations, parking, and shitty, overpriced food."

"Yuri and a couple of NSA guys are waiting for us at the motel. Give me a dollar."

"You need gas money?"

"Just give me the damn dollar."

Jack scrounged through his backpack. "All I got is Bahts." He held out a handful.

Mary grabbed them all. Jack protested. "That's about five bucks US, Jack. That's the cheapest retainer I have been paid since I graduated law school."

"The NSA guys are going to try to encourage you to flee to Russia. Don't. That will discredit you as a Russian spy. Eliminates you as a problem...well, short of eliminating you." Mary made a slicing motion across her neck to further illustrate her point. "Which, trust me, is still on page one in their playbook."

"No good deed. But I am gonna write a strongly worded letter to the agency if they off me now instead of three weeks ago. That's some evil bullshit."

"I'm gonna need you to shut up and look pretty..." She took a look at Jack. "Well, just shut up. Squeeze my leg if you need to talk to me and we will go outside... but let me do the talking. I'm good at this shit. You're a lamb being led to slaughter."

"Thanks for the imagery and the vote of confidence."

"You're welcome. The key is balance. We can't get greedy, and we can't roll over. These guys are prepared to kill you...and me. And I'm too pretty to die."

"Then I sure as hell hope you have a plan B?" Jack said.

"I do. Yuri got me your driver. Some big ifs, though. Did Yuri compromise the driver?" Mary pondered. "What if he leaks the information?"

"First, he had most of the information before I did. Second, I thought of that. There are three encrypted copies with reporters I think I can trust. I have a couple copies hidden back in Afghanistan and I mailed a copy to Barney in Belize."

"Barney? What the hell, Jack. My life is in the hands of that lecher?"

"Judgy, much? He just spectates...mostly. You can count on Barney trading your life for your ass anytime. Perfect choice. No one would think I would be stupid enough to send him something so important," Jack assured her.

"I would," she replied.

"But you have had the rare privilege to have seen me naked."

Mary sighed. "You might want to look up the words rare and privilege, Jack."

"Now you're just being mean."

"I took an oath."

"To tell the truth…"

"No, Jack. I'm a defense lawyer. I'm paid to obviate the truth and to be unpleasant."

"And you are damn good at it I see…at least the mean part."

"We are getting off track here, Jack. We are dealing with the NSA and some black contractors. They could have found all your safety copies," Mary stated the obvious.

"I think they prefer African-American now, Mary."

Mary scoffed. "Black ops, Jack."

"But they will never know for sure they got all the copies, and we will always have Russia."

Mary led Jack into an open-air room covered with palm fronds and facing the ocean. Yuri embraced Jack. "Damn. You made it. That cost me a thousand rubles."

"You bet against me? That kinda smarts, dude."

"Hundred to one odds you would make it, Jack. I could have made a killing. But, like you said, you're an accountant who counts beans in an AC building. Who knew?" Yuri sighed and introduced his boss by his unintelligible Russian name.

Mary's unnamed NSA contact was there and embraced Mary longer than Jack would have liked. A fourth man stayed in the shadows and did not stand or introduce himself. Jack studied him carefully. He was a small man dressed in an expensive suit ill-suited for the situation or climate. His features and manners were unequivocally feminine. He made no facial expressions and, inexplicably, had an air of haughtiness that annoyed the hell out of Jack.

Jack pointed at the man. "If that dude ain't a chick, he missed a damn fine opportunity," Jack said loudly. The Russians cackled, slapping the table. Mary remained grim-faced and pinched Jack's leg as a warning.

As predicted, Mary's NSA contact urged Jack, for his own safety, to flee to Russia. "It's your best option as we see it, Jack."

"We welcome Jack with open arms, we give him sturdy, fertile Russian wife with most…" they looked at each other, smiling, "…some of her teeth, stubborn mule, log cabin with satellite TV, running water in summer, working two-seater outhouse, all vodka he can drink, and hillside farm with just a handful of rocks here and there, just barely in Siberia," Yuri said with an overdone accent, broadly smiling while covertly catching Jack's eye with, what Jack interpreted as, a warning.

"Tempting, Yuri. But I thought your daughters were all married," Jack replied.

"You think we should give you fancy dacha on Black Sea next door to Putin and Anna Kournikova as wife?"

"Tempting offer, but can she cook? And I'll need a recent picture. Russian women tend to put on some weight with age I hear."

To summarize a four-hour dick measuring session full of both overt and covert threats, Mary negotiated a deal Jack was very acquainted with. He would sign an NDA and take a boat load of cash in return. The NDA required Jack to assume a new identity and live outside the US or it's commonwealths for a period of ten years. Jack insisted his first name remain the same. Although social media was still in its infancy, Jack could not have any accounts under any identities. The NSA would classify his file at the highest level on a need-to-know basis. In return, the NSA would deposit ten million in a new, untraceable currency known as Bitcoin into Jack's account immediately and five million on the anniversary of this date for the rest of his life, as long as he did not violate the terms of the NDA. Should Jack violate the NDA, the twist on this agreement was simple…termination…his. Should his life end mysteriously without said violation of the NDA, the data would automatically be released to the worldwide press.

Mary looked at Jack. "You good?"

"Hell no. Why don't they just pay me in Beanie Babies, Cabbage Patch Dolls, or baseball cards? Maybe I can flash my boobs and get Mardi Gras beads."

"Outside, Jack."

Jack obeyed the order and met Mary outside. "What the hell, Jack? Not a fan of crypto? It's the only way we can keep it untraceable."

"Nothing is untraceable," Jack replied. "And I don't want an attic full of Beanie Babies. That shit has no underlying value. And I can't spend it without converting it into cash and then it's just as traceable as if they paid me cash. I had rather have them commission Miss Royal's third grade special ed class to create some artwork and pass off as fine art at some snooty gallery in Manhattan. Nobody questions art. It's like science. Let the Feds find some ass-clowns to buy it with some of their illicit dark money. Works for pedaling influence with politicians. And to be clear, the Feds pay for the crayons and paper."

The NSA finally agreed to a derivative of Jack's payment method although they found it absurd "finger painting" could be passed off as fine art. Little did they know. Mary insisted on $25 million in legal fees. Even Jack raised his eyebrows. "A woman deserves to get paid." The Feds relented. Yuri sighed audibly with relief. The effeminate man in the dark corner pointed his finger at Jack like a gun and winked. Jack blew him a kiss. Mary pinched Jack's leg.

Mary stayed over an extra night. Jack found a VCR rental store that had Casablanca on VHS. Mary had never seen the classic, but she loved it. One night turned into two and then into a week. For some reason neither could attempt to rationalize, Mary and Jack married. The ceremony was a simple one at sunset in Dili on the beach, barefoot and in swimsuits with a couple local kids as witnesses and a local drunk who swore he was a priest.

Mary's office found Jack a place to live and insisted she get back to work. Jack flew to his new home in Montpelier, Uruguay where almost the entire population were descendants from Europeans who fled Europe, mainly the Germanic part, for some mysterious reason shortly after World War II. None were too eager for strangers lurking about regarding ancestral provenance. Jack rented a humble condo on the Rambler, a popular tourist destination, as to not stand out as an American with cash to burn with the Spanish speaking ability of a fifth-grade American kid. It was there he lived out his ten-year exile before moving to Florida to live out a totally different kind of self-imposed exile.

CHAPTER THIRTY-TWO
An Outlaw Wedding

Jack suffered a three-week ordeal while escaping Afghanistan. The ride back from Ocala was exponentially more terrifying. Bank rashly wove in and out of traffic at excessive rates of speed like a man believing himself immortal or one seeking to face his mortality. Safety third. Bank was cross at being sidetracked from his primary mission. Multitasking was not his strong suit. Just short of I-95, Bank nearly sideswiped an Uber. Jack recognized the occupants of the Uber as Barnes and Noble, the rouge FBI agents. Barnes was soundly asleep against Noble's shoulder. Jack ventured to release his death grip and pounded on the Uber's window. Noble appeared agitated as she woke Barnes who pulled his service revolver before opening his eyes. One Eye hurled a full Bud heavy can against the Uber's windshield, forcing the driver off the road and into the ditch. Gaia grabbed One Eye's crotch and worked it like a gear stick. Never was there a purer, more romantical love.

After nearly two hours, the Outlaws and their somewhat tattered passengers arrived at the safe house. Jack resisted kissing the ground. "Where the hell am I and who the hell am I duct-taped to?" Wheels questioned. The drugs were wearing off.

"Both of those are fair questions, Wheels, but for now, let's just say you are in a better place." Jack was second guessing himself on bringing Wheels without his meds. He hoped heroin might serve as an alternative if necessary. Otherwise, Jack would just have to let the Outlaws deal with Wheels. He justified the outcome couldn't be worse than the Bin.

Barnes stormed off into the house, agitated at the delay. Mary sashayed out of the garage like a Southern belle at her debutante. Jack's jaw literally dropped. "Hello, Jack. No Casablanca quotes today?" Mary coyly teased.

"You had me at hello," Jack replied. "You have aged well."

"Pretty sure that's some other romcom, Jack. And that's no compliment. Even so, you, on the other hand, Jack, have put on a few in the middle and lost a little off the top since I have last had the pleasure."

"Missed you too, love. See you gained a couple cup sizes and found a good colorist. I hope you didn't spend all our retirement money on boob jobs, fillers, liposuction, and Botox treatments."

"I do miss our romantical conversations. You do know, Jack, outside of East Timor, I am certain our marriage is not recognized as legal."

"Now that really hurt. I knew I should have never married a lawyer. I see marriage as a more spiritual state...not a matter of state."

"For an accountant, you are quite the philosopher of bullshit."

"You are right. I should leave the bullshit to you professionals...the lawyers."

"On that note, wanna go have some real fun?" Mary asked, demurely placing a perfectly manicured finger mockingly on her cheek.

"Thought you would never ask." Jack pointed to the safe house. "It's been some time. Well, at least for me. But, to be clear and to my credit, I did just recently turn down a valid, rather insistent offer with a woman half my age and twice my size."

Mary shook her head no and pointed to Jack's house.

"Might be a little crowded over there with bad guys, but hell, I'm down to clown in the center ring."

The two sauntered over to Jack's house with Bank and Purdue following. Jack smelled his pits. "I could use a shower."

"You could use an acid dip, a treadmill, and some Rogaine, Jack."

"So I'm not getting laid?"

"What was your first clue?"

Jack walked into his house through the open garage without knocking. Guns were drawn. Threats were made. Mary ignored the guns, adequately rejoined the threats, and plopped down court documents on the granite countertop. "This, gentleman, is Jack Smith..."

Jack did his crazy smile and curtsied. For reasons only known to Jack, he announced in a mentally challenged voice, "I like cherries".

"This man..." Mary pointed and side-eyed Jack before continuing, "... is the rightful owner of the house you have illegally occupied. These papers are a federal court order for you to vacate this house within the hour".

The agents looked at each other, bewildered. Barnes and Noble had yet to arrive after having been waylaid by a well-aimed Bud Heavy. This was not the FBI's A-team.

"You want to lower your penis extensions before we create more paperwork?" Mary requested.

The agents looked at each other, dumbfounded, but grudgingly complied. "The agent in charge is not currently available."

"Yo'! Monkey bitches! Tick tock…58 minutes and counting until you must vacate the premises. I'm assuming that online law degree taught you to read legal documents without someone holding your hand, so read the court order."

Jack scratched his head and looked at Mary. "Monkey bitches? I mean, there is assholes, regular bitches, fuckwads, dickheads, bastards, losers, douchebags, anal douchebags, shitheads, ass lickers, brown nosers, booger eaters, cocksuckers…but you pull monkey bitches out of your ass?" Jack looked at Mary's ass. "For the love of God, you've had that done, as well. Do you have any original parts left on you?"

Mary seethed. "Not now, Jack."

Barnes and Noble stormed through the door, full of piss and vigor, with wicked hangovers after spending a half hour in the sun waiting for a jacked-up truck full of drunk rednecks to pull them out of the ditch while simultaneously screaming, "Let's go, Brandon" at every vehicle that passed. A lot of vehicles passed.

"So we meet again, Jack," Noble quipped.

Jack turned to Mary. "Now I get it. Monkey bitches. You're psychic."

"What the hell you doing in our house?" Barnes demanded.

"I truly hate repeating myself to half-wits and morons." Mary tapped on the papers. "Read."

Barnes read the headlines. "Look, lady..."

Jack interrupted. "Once you get to know her, she's really not that much of a lady."

"Thanks, Jack."

"You're welcome, Mary. I think facts are important here."

"There something you two need to disclose before we go on?" Barnes asked.

"She's not just my attorney, she's my wife, and a damn near cyborg. I would watch my six," Jack replied.

"No, I'm not."

"Potato, potatow."

"If you two lovebirds are done peacocking, I have Jack's signature giving us his permission to use the property as we see fit." Barnes slapped a file down on the counter with undue confidence that Noble had retrieved in the preceding moments.

"May I examine those papers, please?" Mary asked.

"Help yourself, counselor, and then get you and your crazy ass husband the fuck out of my house."

Mary picked up the papers. "Again, not my husband...unless we are in East Timor." Mary looked around dramatically. "We are not in East Timor." She gave a cursory read of the agent's legal paper. Barnes and Noble glanced at each other, perplexed. "Oh, I see. My bad, everything looks in order," Mary continued.

Barnes smiled. Jack's smile spilled over the margins of his face in anticipation of Mary's coup de gras.

"That is..." Mary pointed her manicured nail at the signature line on the papers, "...as long as the property owner is one Mister Shrimp Johnson," her voice rose impishly at the end.

Mary looked at her watch. "Forty-eight minutes, monkey bitches, or my friends back there will burn this place down with whoever the fuck remains within. We clear?"

"Can we not burn my house down?" Jack mumbled.

Bank and Purdue started hysterically laughing. The agents looked at each other in confusion. Mary strutted out of the house while rendering the universal sign of contempt. Jack looked at Noble. "I still owe you, sweet cheeks," and blew her a kiss. "Wait for it, Red. It's coming in spades."

They returned to the safe house just as Apache pulled up with Dakota. "What the holy hell, Dakota?"

"I decided I didn't want to go home. FOMO, I guess," Dakota sheepishly replied.

Jack looked at Apache. Apache shrugged. "She, he, they, them, it…is a persuasive little witch."

Dakota kissed Apache on the cheek. He winced and wiped the cheek with the back of his hand.

"'She' works just fine."

Mary looked at Jack. "Not twice your weight."

Jack laughed. "It's complicated but trust me, she is not the "she" offering me her services. Dakota is nothing to worry about."

Mary took a long look at Dakota before responding. "I wish I shared your confidence."

Wheels came out. Dakota bent down and hugged him tightly. Adversity creates strong ties.

Jack introduced everyone to Mary and Dakota. Mary's level of concern regarding Dakota grew exponentially. Her Spidey sense tingled or, was she truly just jealous, she pondered. Jack on his best day was not much of a catch. This was not his best day. Yet Mary remained conflicted about a man she hardly knew but found his way passed the carefully guarded emotions in her like no other.

Shortly, the FBI abandoned Jack's house. Mary, Jack, Dakota, Purdue, and Wheels moved into the house. The Feds had destroyed it. The bedrooms had been turned into dorms with bunk beds crowded in wall-to-wall fashion. The living areas had been obviously stacked full of surveillance equipment but all that remained were the cables and equipment racks, along with a giant hole in the side of the house pouring in ice cold air. Mary and Jack took what used to be the primary bedroom. Mary suggested Jack fire his housekeeper. Purdue and Wheels shared one guest bedroom and Dakota the other.

The big news over at the safe house was that the crew had sold out of product. The gang thought Bank would be proud...he was furious. "Why the hell didn't you raise the price? There are still two days left. You guys just going to sit around and party?"

"That was the plan, Bank. And to be fair, you were too busy off tilting at windmills to even check in on us peasants."

"Wait...You read Cervantes?"

"Who?"

"The dude who wrote Don Quixote...the quote about windmills."

"Nah, man...heard it on the Simpsons. Tilting windmills...I mean, cows I get, but windmills. Holy hell. Whole 'nother level and cool as shit, right?"

"That tracks. Now get your dumb ass the hell out of my sight." Intelligence proved a liability at times. Ignorance could truly be bliss.

Bank suspected his crew attempted a cursory effort at best to contact him. A lack of product freed the gang members to party. They liked to party. The entire Bike Week had been FUBAR'ed, and he had an ominous feeling it was just going to get worse, even without the Feds babysitting next door. Bank grabbed a couple beers and walked out to the dock to smoke a blunt to escape the madness of the house and gather his thoughts. He spotted One Eye and Gaia on the dock and started to pivot, but calculated, incorrectly, they were likely the lesser of two evils.

One Eye appeared uncharacteristically anxious at Bank's arrival. "You okay, asshole?" Bank asked.

"Marry me, bitch," One Eye replied to Bank with his carefully rehearsed tender proposal.

Bank opened his beer purposely and took a long gulp, emptying half the bottle before replying. "While I'm flattered, One Eye, as a traditionalist, there are still certain rules to the marriage game in my book. One, and foremost, the couple require a different set of both indoor and outdoor plumbing. Not woke yet, I make no such claims nor ambitions. Second, the proposer must get down on bended knee. Seeing you are 0 and 2 and sweating like a smooth-faced cop in county lockup, maybe reconsider your phrasing and hit reset facing that way." Bank pointed toward Gaia.

One Eye nodded aggressively, turned, dropped to one knee, and repeated his proposal without deviation. "Marry me, bitch." It was more a statement than a request. Gaia replied without hesitation and, with the sophistication only Gaia could exhibit. "Fuck you in the ass with a chainsaw, you syphilitic-dicked old man." And their future wedded bliss was bound. They both stripped naked, jumped off the dock, and into the muddy river to mark the occasion, woefully unaware of both its shallow depth and muddy bottom punctuated with razor sharp clamshell beds.

Bank opened a storage bin on the dock looking for something to help fish the lovebirds out of the river. One Eye surfaced first, having the unfortunate luck of crash-landing into a clamshell bed. Blood covered One Eye from just above his knees to his neck. Foolishly, he kept hopping from one foot to the other, continuing to slice his feet open on the sharp edges of the shells. "Get me the hell out of here, Bank."

"Quit jumping around like a circus monkey on fire and swim, asshole," Bank replied. He let the ladder down on the dock.

Knee deep and sinking, Gaia appeared in the muck. She couldn't move and was beginning to panic. But she could talk. The words coming from her mouth were mostly unintelligible but were loud enough to be heard from Ponce Inlet and punctuated by the occasional coherent non-vulgarity. One Eye made no effort to help her. Bank thought this might be the shortest engagement in history.

Bank had located a fishing net that was just long enough to reach her if he leaned out holding onto one of the piers. "When you get free," Bank advised, "... don't try to walk. Swim to the ladder".

"Do I look stupid?" Gaia asked, trapped in waist deep water, covered in mud, and shouting obscenities at her would-be rescuer.

"Rhetorical in nature, I assume," Bank quietly replied.

Contrary to Bank's prediction, after a six-hour visit to Urgent Care for One Eye, the wedding date was set for Saturday. One Eye's wounds were all superficial but abundant and he had lost a lot of blood. The real concern, the nurse practitioner advised, was infection. Bank thought to himself that one night with Gaia just might kill him, then.

One Eye was covered with bandages oozing blood and some green substance that stank of death from his toes to his chest as he approached Bank. "Looking buff, One Eye. You been working out?"

"Thanks, Bank. Feeling it, you know. I'm in fucking love, man."

"Might just be the pain killers and a fifth of Jack, One Eye."

"Yeah, that, too. Anyways Bank...been pondering..."

"Shit, that scares me," Bank interrupted. "Your pondering skills are muted on your best day, and this ain't your best day, One Eye."

"No, man. For real, Bank. Do us the honor and officiate our nuptials."

"Do I look like a preacher, One Eye?"

One Eye surveyed the room. "Closest thing around these parts." One Eye was not wrong.

Wheels, overhearing the conversation, interjected. He pulled out a laptop and within seconds had Bank legally ordained as the good Reverend Bank of The Demon Outlaws. "You are also a legal notary and licensed gun dealer in the state of Florida and Texas, with an application pending in Nevada and Arizona."

Dakota also overheard the conversation and went to locate Gaia. She explained the potential legal problems of One's Eyes plans to have Bank officiate the wedding.

"Like I give a fuck," Gaia responded. "The boy ain't much to look at but he damn sure a natural at cooter munching."

Dakota suppressed her gag reflex. "Just let me get Reverend Mack to come to make it legal and sign the papers," Dakota pleaded.

"Damn, girl. You got a thing for that big piece of dark meat."

"He has just always been good to me. Don't you think it would be good to see him and make sure you're legally married?"

"You do you, boo. Maybe we can make it a double wedding or is it just a friends with benefits kind of arrangement?"

Dakota blushed. "Strictly business."

Wheels wanted to send out E-vites, but One Eye nixed that. "Outlaws don't do E-vites, retard. It'll be word of mouth."

"Okay, it's your funeral," Wheels warned and slammed into One Eye's bandaged knees with his chair.

Bank laughed as One Eye rolled on the floor in pain. "He'll fit in nicely."

The dock served as the wedding venue, with the overflow crowd observing the nuptials from the backyard and on Jack's adjacent dock. Dress code was clothing optional at Gaia's demand. Fortunately, few chose this option. Biker's aren't known to be young or fit. A disdain for light beer and cardio tended to add a few pounds. It was the social event of the season. Some 500 bikers were anticipated. Thousands attended. Bank had the foresight to anticipate the opportunity and arranged an emergency delivery of product that had arrived just hours before the event. Sales were brisk.

Mack drove up minutes before the ceremony and gave Dakota the wedding gift. He joined Jack and delivered the bawdy bride via skiff to the venue. Dakota served dual roles as her best her/him. Mary refused to travel with the wedding party after catching a brief glimpse of the bride's attire: knee-length boots and a white t-shirt where the bride had crudely written in multi-colored crayons, "Eat my hairy cooter". A long veil partially covered her ass but the lion's share of her "lady" parts was on display.

One Eye simultaneously beamed and oozed blood as he looked down on his half-naked bride who was struggling to climb the stairs while holding a makeshift bouquet of Mexican petunias plucked from Jack's backyard. A sudden gust of wind blew Gaia's veil aside, and Jack and Dakota were offered a full view of Gaia's ass where they observed a second two-ply paper veil billowing in the breeze. Dakota grabbed at it but missed. Jack feigned throwing up over the side. "My heart just wasn't in it," Dakota confessed.

Jack made the sign of the cross. "All your sins will be forgiven, my child."

Dakota demurely smiled. "That's really good to know, Jack," she said.

Mack scoffed and disappeared into the crowd as discreetly as a 250-pound black sober man can in a crowd of mostly white drunken bikers. It was akin to the game find Waldo but in reverse.

"We are gathered here on this spring morning to celebrate and mourn the beginning and the end," Bank began in a booming, baritone voice that carried across the river in pleasing waves. "To join these two unholy infidels in a state of matrimony that, by the odds our chapter bookie has calculated so far," Bank pulled a piece of paper from his jeans, "...has the smart money lasting less than three weeks and ending in death by one or both of the parties". The crowd roared. Gaia laughed maniacally. One Eye bled.

"Anyway...Let's get this party started. You..." He pointed to One Eye. "For purposes ambiguous at best, take this clearly insane bitch Gaia to be your lawfully wedded bride?"

"Fucking ehh, Bank. She is smoke."

Bank pointed at Gaia. "You take this equally crazy, worthless, herpes-infested, criminal that might well bleed out before your honeymoon to be your husband?"

"As long as he eats my hairy cooter, I'll marry the bastard."

One Eye knelt on the dock prepared to prove his fealty.

"For the love of God, One Eye, not here," Bank implored.

One Eye reluctantly stood.

"With the power vested in me by the Almighty internet, I pronounce you two circus sideshow freaks, husband and wife. May ye do the universe a solid and never conceive. Let the party commence. Please don't forget to tip your waiters, bartenders, and friendly drug dealers."

Jack had made way back to his dock and joined Mary. "Quite the clientele you attract."

"Glass houses, Jack. The bride's your buddy."

Purdue joined them. "You a part of this shit, man?" Jack asked.

"What the hell makes you think I'm not?" Purdue replied.

Jack poured Purdue a tall glass of Seagram's straight. "I'm an old man." Jack scratched his greying beard as if to illustrate the point. "And, with that comes a certain amount of wisdom, a big gut, erratic sharts, a bald head, ear hair, and a fickled penis."

"And I'm a young man that would like to live to endure an old man's problems."

"Fair enough, but old age is overrated." Jack refilled Purdue's glass. "Take care to not get stranded in purgatory." Jack paused. "You don't belong, do you?"

"Starting shit like that is how you keep a young man from getting old." Purdue downed his whiskey with a flick of his wrist and held out his glass for a refill.

"That's my cue to leave." Mary scurried off the dock.

"Pretty sure that is not a secret, Purdue." Jack pointed to the debauched revelers. "They at least suspect you and you know it. Why else are you sleeping at my house?"

"I like the AC."

Jack scoffed. "Piece of unsolicited advice from an old man who has been in your shoes. Consider yourself already dead. Then you can do what is right without fear of consequences."

"Easy to say for an old man. An accountant, no less.

Jack smirked and raised his glass. "Wasn't always an old man...hadn't been an accountant since you were sporting short britches...and been a dead man for almost as long."

The two sat silent for a few moments. Jack broke the silence. "I hear you worked for big pharma for a spell."

Purdue looked shocked but nodded yes.

Jack continued. "Here is what I know. Big pharma, hell the entire medical complex, is as much about healing as a teenage boy is about romance...a means to an end. It's a long con played well, and the medical complex owns the government. Hardly anyone cares about healing and those who do eventually surrender to peer pressure and the almighty dollar. The medical complex cares about profit and our politicians about power. What do you know? You worked for big pharma and raised the white flag."

"Pretty much the same. Can't prove shit, though. Everyone is brainwashed into thinking the government and the medical system has their best interests at heart.

We are born to trust the government and our doctor. People are sheep, Jack."

"Sapere Aude, Purdue. Let's open some eyes. We can make some noise, shake some trees, kick a few asses..."

"You can't wake the woke. Science is a religion. It's the new opiate for the masses. So, to what end, Jack? A bullet in the head? A dubious car accident? A sudden heart attack? You seem like the type to read Sun Tzu. Don't fight battles you can't win. Know when you lost, Jack, and go gently into that good night. You can't save the world."

"Without the rage? No fucking way, Purdue." Jack was getting drunk. When he drank, he looked back at his life with regret. He never really did anything heinous but, like his childhood pastor once said, "the sins of omission can indeed send you to the fiery pits of hell. What is doesn't always have to be what will be." The two sat in silence for a moment observing the chaos. "One day you will be an old man."

"With friends like you, I highly doubt it."

Jack scoffed and tried a different tactic. "There's an old proverb. I won't give it justice but suffer through it for me. An old man was walking on a beach littered with thousands of starfish that had washed up on the sand. He watched and smiled as a small boy returned a starfish to the ocean. The old man called out to the boy. "There are thousands of those. You can't make a difference."

The boy smiled. "I made a difference to that one," he calmly replied.

Purdue held out his glass to Jack. "I think I might just cry."

"Fuck you, Purdue."

"No, fuck you and your fairytales, Jack. You had your chance. Your time has passed. If you fucked it up, that's on you, old man. Don't look at me as your redeemer."

"Look at you. What are you, an FBI informant? You are not an Outlaw."

"Killing me, Jack. I don't know shit that everyone doesn't already know. The drug companies give incentives to doctors to prescribe their meds. Bonuses if they hit their goals. And rarely do the doctors take the time to understand the efficacy, side effects, or drug interactions of the medication, but you bet your sweet ass they know the incentive rules backwards and forwards. A general practitioner comes out of medical school with a half-million or so in student loans. Doesn't really start earning until they are nearly 30-years-old and, even then, not much over $150,000 a year. What do you expect them to do? The hot cheerleader did not marry them and live in poverty 'til their thirties for their looks." Purdue finished his drink and stood. "Nobody gives a shit about any starfish, Jack. No one really cares about anyone other than themselves. That's the problem."

"Run while you can then, Purdue. You got played. This was never about the Outlaws. Whoever in the government you're working for does not give two shits about your life. But those gents..." Jack pointed at the safe house... "They give a shit. God forgives...Outlaws don't".

"So I've heard."

Jack left Purdue on the dock and walked back toward the house. Mary pointed at the safe house dock where Gaia and One Eye had just dove into the murky water followed by about half the guests. Most of the guests were too inebriated and or uncoordinated to dive successfully and belly-flopped into the shallow water, miraculously remaining relatively unharmed. A few of the more athletic guests dove perfectly into the shallow waters from the top rail, breaking their necks or backs. A merciful quick death, at least. The truly unfortunate were uncoordinated but found the clamshell beds and were cut bow to stern by razor sharp, bacteria riddled edges. A half-dozen juvenile bull sharks took sample bites out of the bikers but were deterred by their unseemly tastes and textures and swam away for a more appetizing meal before doing serious damage. Dozens died. Hundreds were severely injured. It was the wedding of the century. "For the love of God," Jack said as he dialed 911.

CHAPTER THIRTY-THREE
The Last Ride

Meanwhile, in the quaint beach village of Flagler Beach, about 18 miles south on Highway A1A, Barnes and Noble flaunted their FBI creds to break the long line at the Golden Lion to get seated. The patrons reluctantly acquiesced, several already on FBI terrorist watch lists after attending school board meetings. It was a chamber of commerce afternoon, in the mid-seventies with nary a cloud in the sky. A gentle breeze carried the sounds of the Atlantic crashing onto the beach throughout the bar. Overhead, flocks of seagulls and pelicans, also known as nature's trash collectors, made their way south, dropping poop bombs and segregating tourists from locals by the splash patterns on the tourist's uplifted, sun-kissed faces.

The two agents jostled a family of Latinos tightly together to make room onto a picnic table under a

Corona Light umbrella in the sand. A couple of aging rockers, who had surrendered to comfortable footwear and support hosiery, were doing a resolute job covering '70's and '80's rock bands from the adjacent outdoor stage flanked by two weathered concrete lions imploring children to stand clear lest be mauled. The place was packed with mostly biker wannabes and a few blue-haired locals, most of whom were transplants from northern states seeking sunshine, freedom, and lower taxes. The one-percenters were largely absent as they were attending the blessed nuptials.

The Pricklepants, a recent transplant couple from New England, were dressed as pirates. Billy Bob was a recently retired rocket scientist, gifted painter, and an all-around Renaissance man. Now he spent his days as a starter at a local private golf course and moonlighted during season at tourist hangouts as a pirate for shits and giggles and a little extra pocket change. He wore an authentic leather eye patch, a replica swashbuckling sword honed with undue care capable of slicing limbs, and a self-designed, realistic hook that was also capable of inflicting deadly wounds. Charlotte (who preferred to be called "Charlie") was able to track him by the large metal balls dangling from his leather belt that pealed to the rhythm of his gait. His trousers were striped, wool, and neatly tucked into his leather boots. His attention to detail was noteworthy. Charlie was a full-time volunteer. A good-hearted woman with a difficult past, she filled her days between the food bank, the church, her Ladies Club, and girl scouts. She was a devout Catholic and gave no quarter to those who violated the big ten as outlined on the stone tablets toted down the mountain by the bearded man in the flowing robe. She was dressed as a beer wench with a tight leather corset and, for effect, shouldered her pet Macaw. The bird added character and authenticity by littering her shoulder with bird seed and her back with bird poo. She sported a self-designed pirate hat that doubled as a bird feeder. Tucked inside her boots was an authentic dagger. The pirated duo ambled through the crowd and posed for pictures for tips and free drinks. Billy Bob had 101 pirate jokes, none of which were remotely funny to anyone not three sheets into the wind. Billy Bob got a lot of laughs. Ironically, the best tips came when Charlie threw drinks in patrons faces after an inappropriate comment or pass. People appreciate authenticity and she was authentically pissed. Those who dared challenge her were met with the tip of Billy Bob's blade. A lot of Instagram posts were produced, and the pair became somewhat of a local legend.

The pirates approached Barnes and Noble. "Piss off, goddamn it," Barnes growled.

Charlie, of course, did not cotton to such use of the Lord's name and was primed for instances when belligerent patrons foolishly took His name in vain. She produced a motel-sized bar of soap procured for such occasions and deftly crammed it into Barnes' mouth. Noble laughed hysterically while falling into the sand. Barnes pulled his service revolver but smartly re-holstered the weapon as he faced a group of patrons with guns aimed in his direction and no less than 20 red laser lights trained between his eyes. Terrorist list or not, Florida is a stand your ground state. The band never missed a beat of Stairway to Heaven as the crowd returned to merriment. Florida! Many a northerner will comment they love Florida but hate Floridians. But one simply cannot separate the two. The quirky, independent, freedom-loving nature of Floridians makes the state what it is. There is already a state for New Yorkers. It is called New York. There's even one for the self-righteous New York City folk on a budget. It's called New Jersey. The influx from this part of the country caused a change in the unofficial Florida motto from "Hold My Beer" to "Don't New York my Florida".

Barnes brusquely snagged a harried waitress with a snarky attitude and ordered two double-chilled tequila shots. The waitress scoffed. "We don't serve sorority girls at this bar during Bike Week." Noble discreetly pulled out her FBI credentials. The waitress replied, "Or assholes," and walked off, displaying the .380 affixed to her hip. This was Flagler County. Everyone carried. Most everyone rightfully held a deep mistrust for the Feds in all of their innumerable three letter permutations. As Ronald once said, the most feared words ever are: "We are here from the government and want to help".

The Latino family had a bottle of cheap tequila and amicably shared a shot with the two agents. "You drink this donkey piss warm?" Barnes asked. "Yo, hombre, sack up and be grateful," the 15-year-old daughter replied. Noble, after three shots of free tequila, each tasting less and less like donkey piss, looked into Barnes' bloodshot eyes, and said what they had both been thinking. "We been played, cabron. This was never about the Outlaws." Tequila brings out the Spanglish in gringos.

"Maybe. But then who?" Barnes asked.

"Jack."

"Pshaw! That senile old fool? He is just a pawn in a larger game."

"We are the pawns, Noble. Jack is the Rey. Remember his file. It was heavily redacted, yet that newbie tech had it readily available. Conveniently, it was his house that was perfect for a surveillance house. His wife just so happened to be the Outlaws' abogada. Too many coincidences. We got set up to fail, they knew we would go balls to the wall and skip protocol. That, mi amigo, is why they picked us to use as cover for whatever the real mission is."

"So you believe this is some crazy, government conspiracy to take Jack out? Makes no sense. He is a nut job, a drunk, a loser, and tried to kill himself."

"But did he? His name is Jack Smith. Who in the hell is named Jack Smith? He is rich, the government is interested. The hair on my back is standing up," Noble said.

"You have hair on your back," Barnes grimaced.

"Figuratively, pendejo. But probably more than you have on your balls."

"For the record, I manscape on a regular basis. So now we go save Jack? Not good for our careers."

"Why? With your lame ass game, do you really expect visitors? And what careers? The FBI thinks we are a joke and we have been set up as the scapegoats for any fallout. And besides...I don't like getting played."

"Yo, bro," the elder Latino man addressed Barnes as Barnes poured himself another shot. "How about you order a bottle for the table?"

Barnes belligerently signaled the snarky waitress to come over. "Your finest bottle of tequila for our friends from south of the border."

She smiled coyly. "No problem, Senor. I am here to serve your every need above everyone else in this crowded bar. We have one bottle of Patron Tequila Extra Anejo en Lalique Serie II in reserve for just such a special occasion for our most favored customers."

"Nothing is too good for my new amigos," Barnes confidently replied.

"And so it shall be." The snarky waitress smiled broadly and bowed demurely before returning to the bar. Even a dullard should have spotted the waitress' behavioral clues as suspect. Barnes and Noble held law degrees and were highly trained FBI agents and thought nothing of it. Education equates to a false sense of superior intelligence but rarely into itself conveys to wisdom.

The Latino family, on the other hand, looked at each other in shock, but the eldest put his finger to his lips. The waitress returned asking for Barnes' credit card of which he handed over without a second thought as it was government issued. The pirates returned with the bottle and most of the wait staff carrying sparklers and singing, "for he is a jolly good fellow". The McCaw squawked, fluttered his clipped wings, and shit on Barnes' loafers.

Charlie sat the tequila on the table and whispered in Barnes' ear, "I hear this tequila pairs well with bar soap". She crossed herself and whispered to God, "Forgive my sins of ire toward your most imprudent of children".

The snarky waitress returned with the check with a 20-percent gratuity and a 3-percent credit card usage fee added that totaled just north of $10,000. "It's been my pleasure to serve you, Mr. and Mrs. Barnes. Is there anything else I can help you with?" It was the universal "fuck you" reply of anyone in customer service who had done little to nothing and could not care less.

"You could chill it..." he responded to her retreating back side.

Noble glanced at the check. "This dump serves $10,000 bottles of tequila. That is going to be tough to get by accounting."

Barnes was busy checking the internet. "Damn! I guess they do."

Noble was unmoved. She had accepted her career was dead. "Now that is settled, let's go save that asshole Jack."

"To hell with that. What are they gonna do…fire us? I am drinking at least a shot of this tequila." Barnes, too, had accepted his fate.

The Latino elder snatched the bottle away from Barnes. "You sip this tequila, cabron. You are like an entitled gringo at a border town watching a victim of sex trafficking fuck a donkey. You feel superior with your tiny pee-pee erection in your khaki shorts and smedium polo t-shirt watching the abuse, but you are insignificant and helpless and need to feel superior watching the humiliation of others. Vaya con dios y ahora ala chingada, punta."

Barnes poured a glass of the expensive tequila and poured it down his throat. "I am superior, you wet back mother fucker."

Billy Bob unsheathed his very real blade and held it to Barnes' throat, nicking his freshly shaven skin. "Ahh, matey. Time to walk the plank." Barnes sharted loudly. The Latino family both gagged and giggled based primarily on their proximity to the incident.

Charlie waved a disapproving finger at the Latino. "Language, Senor." She kept her dagger sheathed but at the ready.

Cell cameras clicked, instas were posted. Billy Bob and Charlie went viral once again as Barnes and Noble hastily retreated.

CHAPTER THIRTY-FOUR
Final Chapter

Barnes drove the rented Prius back to the safehouse at breakneck speeds approaching 50 mph. There was a headwind. Noble rolled the windows down and monitored the police scanner and noted hundreds of calls from the safe house address. Barnes floored the Prius and it accelerated by 5 mph to 55 mph in just over a minute. A flock of seagulls spoiled the windshield making Noble wonder out loud if in fact cows did fly and caused Barnes to swerve off the road and into the dunes.

"Fucking flying dinosaurs." Barnes got out and lifted the car back onto the road with Noble still in the passenger seat.

"I stand corrected. Dinosaurs," Noble mumbled.

The pirates followed the agents on Charlie's hunch she would be needed. Billy Bob protested. Tips were good and would only get better after the confrontation. Charlie shushed him. With the move to Florida, Charlie had found her sea legs.

The two agents arrived at a chaotic scene of emergency vehicles carting off hundreds of near drowning victims but with no immediate sign of Jack. Jack and Mary had taken the newlyweds in the safe house's speed boat away from the carnage and the certain all-night questioning from the police. Dakota jumped in the boat at the last minute. Barnes spotted Jack and the newly betrothed couple as they were leaving and commandeered Jack's john boat to give futile chase.

Just beneath the Halifax Bridge, Dakota produced Reverend Mack's wedding present for the newlywed couple. After chambering a round, she pointed their 9 MM gift at them and convinced the newlyweds to go for a swim. One Eye, still oozing from his earlier wounds, meekly protested. Dakota offered to end his suffering. Gaia exclaimed, genuinely surprised, "Well, eat my cooter. Ginger does have balls," before plunging into the dark, choppy waters.

"Not what I had planned on diving into on my wedding night," One Eye muttered and followed Gaia into the river.

The pirates arrived on the chaotic scene as the boats sped off from the docks. Charlie correctly assessed the situation and had Billy Bob appropriate a boat off a nearby dock as pirates are inclined to do. Billy Bob was an accomplished kayaker but had little experience with motorboats. Charlie got seasick in the tub. The pirate duo quickly managed to spot the newlyweds in the river and drag them into the boat after running over them three times. "Avert your eyes, Billy Bob. This poor, sweet innocent thing has lost her pants."

"Fuck off, old lady," Gaia replied.

Charlie unsheathed her dagger and pushed Gaia back into the water with its tip applied to her forehead. One Eye sat, quietly waving at Gaia spouting expletives in the water, as Billy Bob attempted to navigate the boat in chase of the agents. "Am I going to have trouble out of you, mister?" Charlie asked.

"No, ma'am," One Eye quickly replied. One Eye lamented the likely loss of his bride by drowning, shark, or Loch Ness monster, but was comforted by the fact he had taken the over and death of one or both spouses on the Outlaw bet pool.

Jack was perplexed. Mary less so. Meanwhile, Barnes and Noble gave futile chase in Jack's hijacked john boat. Dakota noticed the following boats and insisted Jack increase the speed. He did as instructed, scouting ahead for obstructions in the water to create a diversion. "What the living hell, Dakota?" Jack asked.

"It's complicated," she replied.

Mary scoffed. "Not really, Jack. She works for the bad guys."

"Bullshit. You have got to stop watching Discovery ID, Mary. How is that possible? And who the hell are the bad guys? Can we all agree to start wearing uniforms where I can at least follow the game?"

Mary hugged Jack. "It's always the ones you least expect, Jack."

A tear fell from Dakota's eye. "I really do like you, Jack. You have been a good friend."

"I feel a "but" coming here. I do so hate buts. They always negate all the good shit you said before it. And to be clear, it's been my life's experience that friends rarely shoot one another...unless they catch them screwing their significant others...Can I rule that out, at least?" Jack looked between Mary and Dakota.

Dakota gave Jack a blank stare. Mary gave him a middle finger. "I'm starting to want her to shoot you."

Jack replied, first to Mary. "Let's put a pin in that, shall we?" He then turned to Dakota. "Then why in God's name are you pointing a very expensive pistol at me?" Jack asked.

"Because I get paid to put you down. It's my job."

"And there is the "but". Well, at least it is good to know to some millennials have found a work ethic. There is that. I trust it is a lot of money, Dakota. Now here is my but. Not for my sake, but yours. But it has been my experience the type of people you are working for don't like loose ends. You, my sweet, innocent child are said loose end. They will come after you, as well."

Barnes and Noble's boat grew smaller and smaller as the more powerful boat pulled away.

"And about Mary?" Jack asked.

"Collateral damage, I am afraid," Dakota replied, shrugging her shoulders.

"Yeah. Mary is kinda a bitch."

"Thanks, Jack."

Jack nodded and waved his hands down as if to say let me handle this, Mary. "Just for curiosity's sake, are you really a tranny?"

"That's offensive, Jack."

"Sorry but not sorry. I am not woke. But, then again, you are about to shoot me and that's not offensive? This PC shit has gotten out of hand, don't you think? Words are more offensive than actions? Give me a fucking break."

"Well, if you must know…"

"Inquiring minds and all."

"Yup, I am all in." She made a chopping motion with her fingers. "I am a woman. Inside and out."

Jack flinched. "So much for follow the science but good on you to own that shit. Spit-balling here, but not a Dave Chappelle fan?"

Dakota frowned. "He is a shit stain on the world."

"So what would that make you, what, a paid assassin, then? Never mind. Rhetorical question. Just do me a solid. Mary is a professional. Just toss her cyborg ass overboard. She has a built-in life jacket now." Jack grabbed his chest simulating Mary's oversized boob job.

Mary had slowed the boat while Dakota was distracted, and Barnes and Noble were almost astride.

"Thanks, Jack. It's only a half mile to shore."

"But you still got nice tits. Some fisherman will save you. If not, them tits will serve as a life vest."

"Always the romantic. Now I remember why I fell for you," Mary retorted, flashing a sarcastic smile.

"Not my piercing grey eyes, chiseled body, ruggedly handsome face, quick wit, and lovemaking skills?"

Mary smirked. "On your best day, you never could compete with my nightstand's inventory." Jack visibly winced as he recalled Mary's nightstand inventory consisted of a backscratcher, pack of tissues, and a Vick's inhaler. "And" Mary continued, "as far as the other traits…time has not been kind to you, Jack".

"Ouch. You know I'm about to die here. Can you throw me a bone?"

"Sorry. Sworn officer of the law, Jack."

"And you choose this moment to grow a conscience?"

Dakota noticed the ploy. "Nice try." Shaking, she pointed the gun at Jack's midsection. Jack grimaced. "Oh, hell no. I'll drown or get eaten by sharks." He pulled the barrel of the gun to his forehead.

"Wait, what? There are sharks in these waters? And I'm supposed to swim to shore?" Mary asked.

Jack held up his finger to Dakota. "Hold that thought. Yes, Mary. Where did you go to school, upstate New York? This the intracoastal. Sharks, dolphins, rays, the entire menu of sea life finds its way up here. But not to worry. I'm sure they will show professional courtesy to a fellow shark."

"So original."

"Under a tiny bit of stress here, Mary. Not at my best."

Jack turned back to Dakota and pulled the gun back to his forehead. "Mary is going to jump overboard now, and you are going to let her go. Your NSA friends will protect you. And besides, she likely will get eaten by sharks which, all in all, is pretty ironic."

"I thought my employer was going to kill me a minute ago?" Dakota asked

"Just trying to get you to change teams." Jack could not help himself. "Again," he added. Dakota used her free hand to show her contempt for Jack's attempt at humor. "Like I said, not at my best."

Jack knew that was a lie. Dakota would be assassinated the minute she returned to shore. He stared directly into her eyes as he heard Mary make the plunge into the dark water while Dakota was distracted. Barnes and Noble swiftly gathered her up. "Hurry," Mary pressed the agents. "Dakota is going to kill Jack."

"But why?" Barnes asked.

Mary sobbed. "Because Jack is a good man and knows to much about the corruption of your government."

Barnes and Noble exchanged glances in the dark. "And I thought we were the good guys," Noble whispered.

Barnes lamented. "Everyone does but rarely is anyone. We pray to the same God for victory. How confusing must that be for the old, bearded fellow. I don't know who I am anymore. Deeper and deeper I follow this hole of rabbits down through the twisting damp earth." Barnes, without further warning, pulled his service revolver out and shot himself in the temple. Noble stifled a scream and scampered to the far end of the boat. Mary grabbed the helm, holding out hope for Jack for reasons beyond her understanding as she continued the chase. She loved the fat, old, bald bastard and began to dream of a quiet life with him on a deserted beach.

The shot's echo reverberated down the river, further unnerving Dakota. She was shaking almost uncontrollably. Jack was worried she would miss, and gut shoot him after all and just prolong his suffering in the water. He locked eyes with her. "Listen, you are doing me a solid. I am tired of running. I am old. I am lost. The world is fucked. You can have it. Frankly, you deserve it. I forgive you. May you live in interesting times." Jack closed his eyes and began singing quietly:

"T'was grace that taught my heart to fear
And grace, my fears relieved
How precious did that grace appear
The hour..."

Epilogue

For years he was invisible like so much of the homeless population. Stains on the landscape to be overlooked, ignored, or painted over until they couldn't hold another coat. The gaunt old man was bald but for a few sprigs of long gray hair he kept covered by a hood. His skin was the color and texture of worn leather from living the last few years on the beach. The old man placed his makeshift tent under a walk over at Flagler Beach north of the pier, away from the tourist scene so as not to be a blight on the town nor be disturbed by the police. His clothes were tattered and salty. Most of his face was grossly disfigured and he was limited to but a singular crystal blue eye that later would be described as ethereal.

According to his faded hospital wristband, his name was John Doe. He had virtually no long-term mental capacity yet saw the world in vivid colors. Maybe it was the drugs the visiting social worker brought weekly or perhaps a happy coincidence of his brain injury, but John Doe had found peace in blissful ignorance of the shit show that surrounded him. The social worker was kind and looked familiar. A petite redhead, she was named after a state John recalled, but never remembered which one, nor did he guess the same one twice. She never corrected him.

During the day, John remained in his carefully organized abode sleeping the day away, reading discarded books or discreetly watching carefree beachgoers as they hurried by his tent to avoid the deadly contagion that was the homeless virus. Occasionally a dog would sniff him out and share his space until the owner would abruptly intervene in horror. John longed for the company of a dog. One cool morning, John awoke to a foul smell and the warm body of an emaciated, mixed-breed, black dog curled against him. The dog's face was asymmetrical with one canine that did not fit into his snout, creating a peculiarly fierce appearance. The dog was without a collar, and no one came to search for him. After a couple days, John dared name the dog Jaws and they bathed in the ocean.

At night, John came to life, first dumpster-diving for scraps of food of which he generously shared with Jaws and the sea birds which cautiously accepted Jaws as no threat. And then John danced. Regardless of weather, all night John danced under the stars at the edge of the surf by the faint light of the moon surrounded by seabirds. Jaws joined in for brief spells and surfed the waves for others, but he mostly napped. When the mood struck, John sang in a booming voice the only song he remembered, Amazing Grace. And when the spirit struck, Jaws howled in perfect harmony. On rare occasion, the seabirds seemed to squawk the chorus.

It began slowly. A few beachside locals investigating the noise, but it grew. Soon there were dozens, then hundreds, of locals nightly sitting in the sand watching the bizarre dance of the madman and his dog in the surf. At first the story went viral on social media, then on mainstream media. Shortly, on full moons, the crowds grew to thousands. The madman and his dog had become a tourist destination. VRBO beachfront rentals even listed their property's proximity to John's performance.

The sleepy beach village debated what to do with John. His devotees left food, water, blankets, cash, flowers, talismans, stone graffiti, notes, dog treats and liquor outside his shelter in hope of some blessing or revelation not to come. Many residents and visitors considered him a local treasure, a prophet. Others scoffed and would argue he was more akin to the village idiot. Still others, more practical in nature, considered him just a golden goose for business. Half the city council considered him a nuisance, the other half a blessing. John was offered a modest, rent-free mobile home. He smiled but refused. Lead with the honey. He was then offered a rent-free jail cell. Follow with the stick. He smiled but again politely refused. The council misread the room trying to insert logic into an illogical argument. The police chief broke the stalemate with two simple words: risk, reward. John subsequently stayed on the beach, unmolested by the authorities.

He ate bits of the gifted food. The rest the birds and Jaws shared eagerly, at times creating an unwelcome outburst of noise and shit bombs. John asked the visiting social worker to take the money and use it to help the other homeless on her route and to by herself a new van.

He drank the liquor while reading the notes left by his devotees. There was never too much liquor although he did share occasional nips with Jaws who had come to him with a taste for Jack Daniels. The occasional storm washed away the rest. At night, John danced while searching his memory, straining to recall the countless prayer requests from that day while searching the sky in the void between the stars for answers to questions he had yet to fully form. And the people watched, silently mesmerized by his ethereal aurora, bizarre rhythmic motions, and herculean stamina…waiting for a revelation that would never come.

Mary's CIA contact forwarded her a social media post about John without context. She booked a flight to Daytona and Ubered out to Flagler Beach. She held the car door open. John was easy to spot. He was in the surf surrounded by a dog, the sea, birds and hundreds of people, dancing as if no one was there. In the dark, she couldn't be certain until the man broke out in a familiar song:

"T'was grace that taught my heart to fear
And grace, my fears relieved
How precious did that grace appear
The hour…"

The dog started howling in remarkable harmony. The birds squawked. The full moon broke out from behind the clouds and illuminated a group familiar to Mary just on the edge of the tide: Dakota, Mack, Noble and Purdue. It was transcendent. A tear rolled down her cheek as she stepped back into the car and whispered to herself, "purgatory, poor Jack, purgatory".

A few months later, a package arrived at Mary's office. She noticed the dimensions and weight of the box as well as the post mark and shut her office door. Inside, she found a short note from Dakota. "These last few years, I have cared for Jack posing as a social worker. It's a small penance I pay not worthy of my sins, but I hope you may one day find it in your heart to forgive me. Know that Jack passed his last few years in blissful peace. I have taken the liberty of taking Jack's dog under my care." A solitary tear stained the note as Mary lifted Jack's earthly remains from the cardboard box.

Mary soon discovered she was the sole beneficiary of Jack's will. Through a multitude of lucrative severance packages, government hush money, smart investing and a thrifty lifestyle, Jack had accumulated nearly $300 million in assets over his lifetime. Mary used the funds to purchase the Pines. Her first order of business was to fire the entire staff in person after a lengthy 4-hour speech providing the staff excruciating details of all their wrongdoings with a bonus 2-hour follow-up for Steph and team. Mary provided a grand finale just as Steph's high-heel was an inch off the property by immediately imploding the building. In its place, Mary built a state-of-the-art, nonprofit, mental healthcare facility. The remaining funds were endowed to the hospital to provide low cost and high-quality care for the mentally ill. To ensure no patient was ever made to feel less than human again, she hired Dakota to oversee a patient advocacy board with carte blanche power over the hospital's administration. The hospital refused any government funding, thus avoiding the nonsensical bureaucracy, treating the elderly and poor for free.

Shrimp Johnson's Memorial Care opened in the spring of 2025. There were no speeches. Just the roar of thousands of motorcycles, a decommissioned morgue van, and a garbage truck, along with the silent purr of a single Prius. On that day, Jack ascended from Purgatory to his rightful place at the side of Odin in Valhalla and the breeze carried his last whispered words…Sapere Aude.

"...the test of a civilization is the way that it cares for its helpless members." – Pearl Buck, first American woman to be awarded both the Pulitzer and Nobel Prizes for literature (pearlsbuck.org).

"We are fucked." – D Malone McMillan

In loving memory of my mother and her siblings, the Meders family, who had little more than a pot to piss in, asked for nothing more, and would share it with anyone in need. And to my father, misunderstood as fathers so often are, rarely granted the same grace as mothers; may we find peace in Valhalla.

CPSIA information can be obtained
at www.ICGtesting.com
Printed in the USA
LVHW072357201222
735667LV00016B/374